HAUTEVILLE HOUSE
MUSEUM GUIDE

PARIS musées

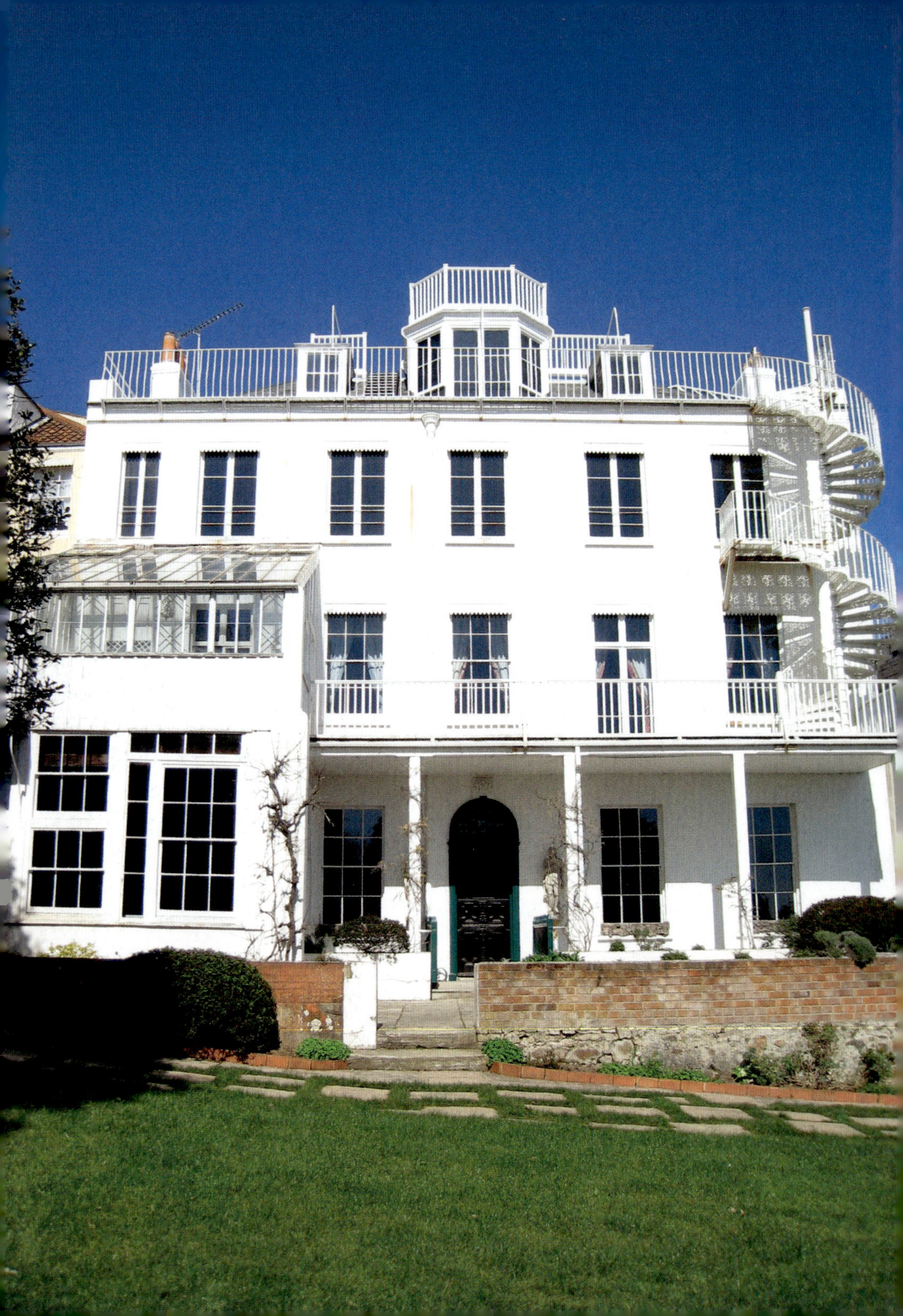

Contents

6 **Foreword**
Danielle Molinari

12 **Victor Hugo and the Channel Islands**
Gérard Pouchain

22 **Hauteville House**
Leïla Jarbouai

24 **Ground floor**
25 The hall and waiting room
28 The billiard room
31 The tapestries room
34 The studio/smoking room
37 The faience corridor
38 The dining room

44 **First floor**
46 The red drawing room
49 The blue drawing room
52 The conservatory

54 **Second floor**
57 The oak gallery
61 The landing/library

64 **Third floor**
65 The antechamber
67 The lookout
70 Victor Hugo's bedroom

74 **The garden**

80 **Appendices**
80 Learn more
83 Timeline
86 Practical Information

N.B.: Except where mentioned, the works reproduced belong to the collection of the Maison de Victor Hugo in Paris.

Hauteville House façade viewed from the garden

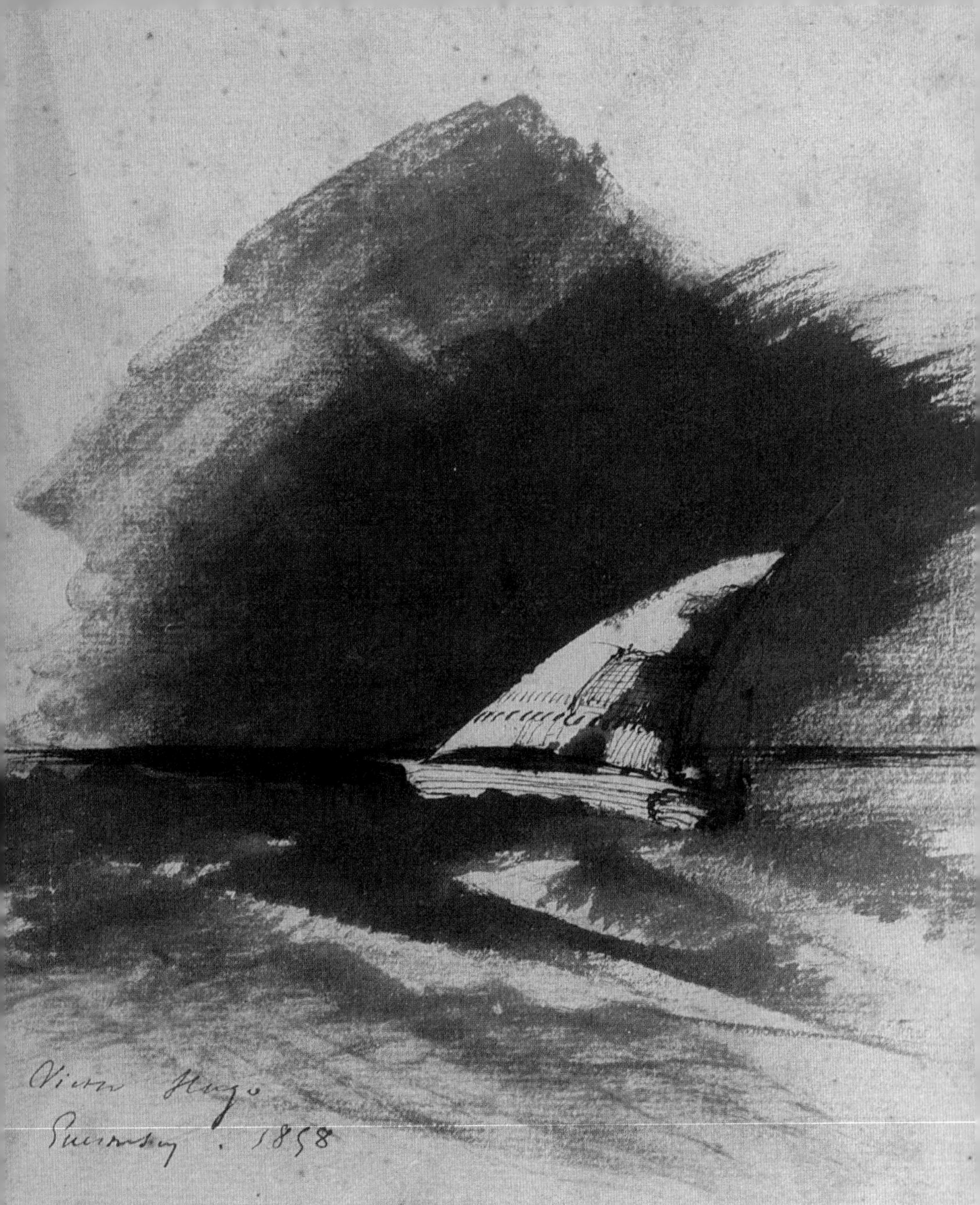

EXIL

Foreword

'I'm told that you are living in a high-perched and poetic residence resembling your spirit, and that you are happy in the din of wind and water.'

Charles Baudelaire to Victor Hugo, 27 September 1859

ill. 1
Victor Hugo
(1802–85)
"Exile" or *Sailing Boat*
Pen, brush or feather brush and brown ink on watermarked verge paper
23.7 x 15.8 cm
Mounted in a copy of the first edition of *Contemplations* (Paris, Michel Lévy-Pagnerre, 1856) vol. II
MVHP-D-138

If ever a house could be rightfully called 'la Maison de Victor Hugo', then it is Hauteville House on Guernsey. The writer acquired this large house looking out over the ocean, decorated and furnished it throughout, and of course spent fifteen years of his exile there.

In August 1856, he wrote to Jules Janin: 'No longer having a homeland, I want to have a roof.' And for that roof he was obliged to pay the yearly 'poulage' tax, which consisted in giving two fowls or an equivalent sum of money to the lord of the manor, thereby protecting him from being expelled – as he had been from Belgium and Jersey. Becoming a house owner also encouraged Hugo to put down new roots, and the deprivation which exile inexorably caused must have been at least partially allayed when, after long months of work, he saw his house gradually become the mirror of the inner universe of a poet who, perhaps more than any other, was 'a world enclosed within a man'.

Baroque, dark, luminous, mysterious, ostentatious but always surprising, Hauteville House became the pantheon of the 'Ego Hugo' inscribed amidst the coats-of-arms and countless maxims, usually in Latin, subtitling the house's profuse and composite décor and telling us some of the exiled poet's thoughts on his condition, mankind, people, life, death, day, night, passing time, the soul, the spirit, love, faith and God.

Charles immediately saw his father's decoration of the house for what it was: a work of art in its own right, 'a veritable three-storey autograph, something, if you will permit the word, like a poem in several rooms.' Adèle watched her husband nostalgically and uneasily settle into exile. On 17 October 1856, she wrote to Mme Paul Meurice: 'So here we are in our new house; for me it's like a statement of exile. It is as if the hope of ever living near you has vanished [...] Into this one my husband is putting his gildings, his wall hangings, all his fantasy and all his care. Here we are again hanging on the walls. We are spending a lot of money...'

Turning a deaf ear to complaints and even threats – François-Victor having said to him, 'Your house is yours. We'll leave you alone in it.'– Hugo, for his part, was satisfied with the end result. He wrote to Viollet-le-Duc: 'It's a pity I'm a poet, what an architect I would have made!' And during the last years of exile, he even allowed tourists to visit the house. He wrote in his diary on 19 October 1867: 'Apparently, Marie [Marie Sixty, their servant] has earned herself more than 200 francs showing the house to the curious during my absence'. The next day, in a letter to François-Victor, he wrote: 'This summer we have had nearly one thousand foreign visitors to Hauteville House.' The house was already a museum before officially becoming one.

In 1862, when work was completed on the house's crowning glory, the glass and steel 'lookout' on the roof, was completed, its creator proudly commissioned Edmond Bacot to take photographs of the residence. Hugo sometimes appears in these pictures, notably in the 'large, deep, mysterious' garden, a distant echo of the one at Impasse des Feuillantines and his 'blond childhood, alas, too fleeting'. These priceless photographic testimonies also show us how little it has changed since.

The links between Hauteville House and Hugo's writing are manifold. Firstly, *Contemplations* enabled him to buy it: '*Contemplations* will pay for everything,' he wrote to Jules Janin on 16 August 1856. But also in Hugo's decoration of the house, which sometimes echoes works predating his exile, and must have given him the impression of being a little bit 'at home'. The 'Nostre-Dame de Paris' portal was inspired by Célestin Nanteuil's frontispiece for the new edition of the novel in 1833. This obligatory entrance via the Middle Ages confirms Victor Hugo's enduring taste and adds a sombre, grave touch to the ensemble, its nocturnal facet one could say, whereas its diurnal facet is its radiant references to Far-Eastern art. The silk damasks, beaded tapestries, carpets and gilded panelling in the red and blue drawing rooms are reminiscent both of *Orientalia* and *Autumn Leaves.*

Although he sometimes found solitude hard to bear, Hugo was fully aware of the enrichment it brought to his work, which flourished considerably during his exile. It was during this period that he finished the first part of *The Legend of the Ages* (1859) and *Les Misérables* (1862), wrote *William Shakespeare* (1864), *The Toilers of the Sea* (1866), that novel so steeped in the life of the island and the contemplation of 'this immense dream of the ocean', and then *The Man Who Laughs* (1869). He also wrote *Free Theatre* there, his first return to the theatre since the flop of *The Burgraves*. And produced some of his finest drawings, including *Justitia* (1857), the three large *Lighthouses* (1866), and innumerable seascapes and ships battling with the elements, which he saw as a metaphor for his own combat.

On 14 June 1927, twenty-four years to the day after the inauguration of the Maison de Victor Hugo in Place des Vosges, the City of Paris became official owner of Hauteville House thanks to the generosity of the writer's descendents: Jeanne, and the children of her brother Georges, Jean, Marguerite and François. The City of Paris was now

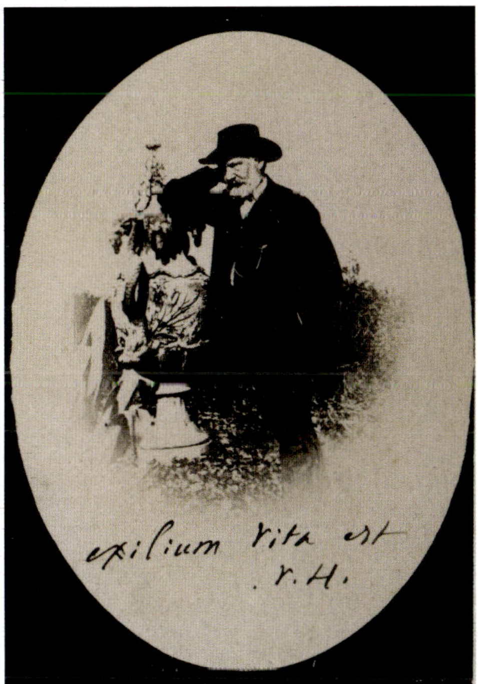

ill. 2
Arsène Garnier
(1822–1900)
Victor Hugo leaning against the fountain in the garden of Hauteville House;
Victor Hugo's hand writing "Exilium Vita Est. V. H".
Albumen print
10.2 x 6.2 cm
MVHP-PH-3122

trustee of the two places where Victor Hugo lived the longest, and whose peerless and diverse collections complement one another wonderfully.

Hauteville House is still haunted by the genius of its former owner and seems to have been 'envisioned' in much the same way as Gilliat's house in *The Toilers of the Sea*, but by Hugo this time. And in the hall, on the right wall, opening on the billiard room, attentive visitors will also notice the word of greeting spoken by their host: *AVE*.

Danielle Molinari
Chief Curator
Director, Maison de Victor Hugo and Hauteville House

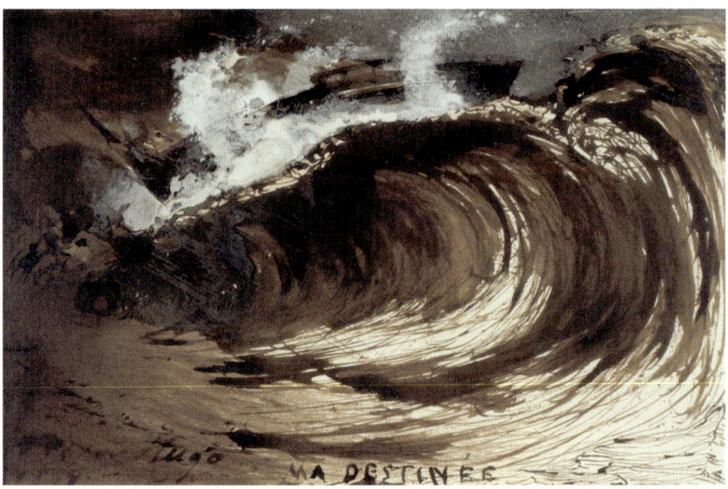

ill. 3
Victor Hugo
(1802–85)
My Destiny, 1867
Pen, paintbrush, use of feather barb and brown ink, white gouache, with paper cut-out impression on vellum paper
17.4 x 25.9 cm
MVH-D-927

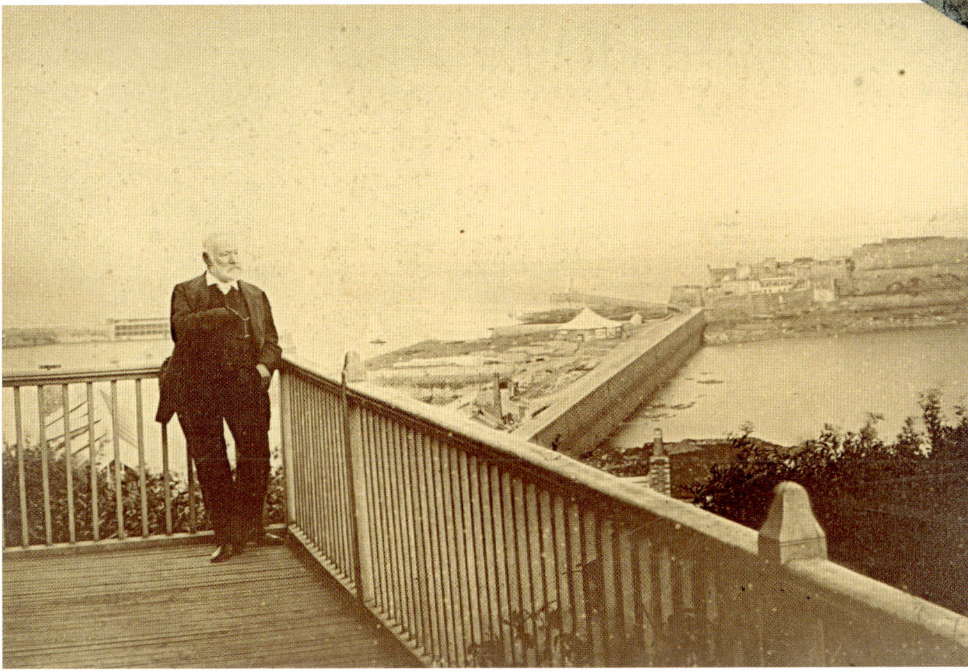

ill. 4
André
Victor Hugo leaning against the balustrade on the terrace at Hauteville House,
1878
Albumen print
8.3 x 6.3 cm
MVHP-PH-2277

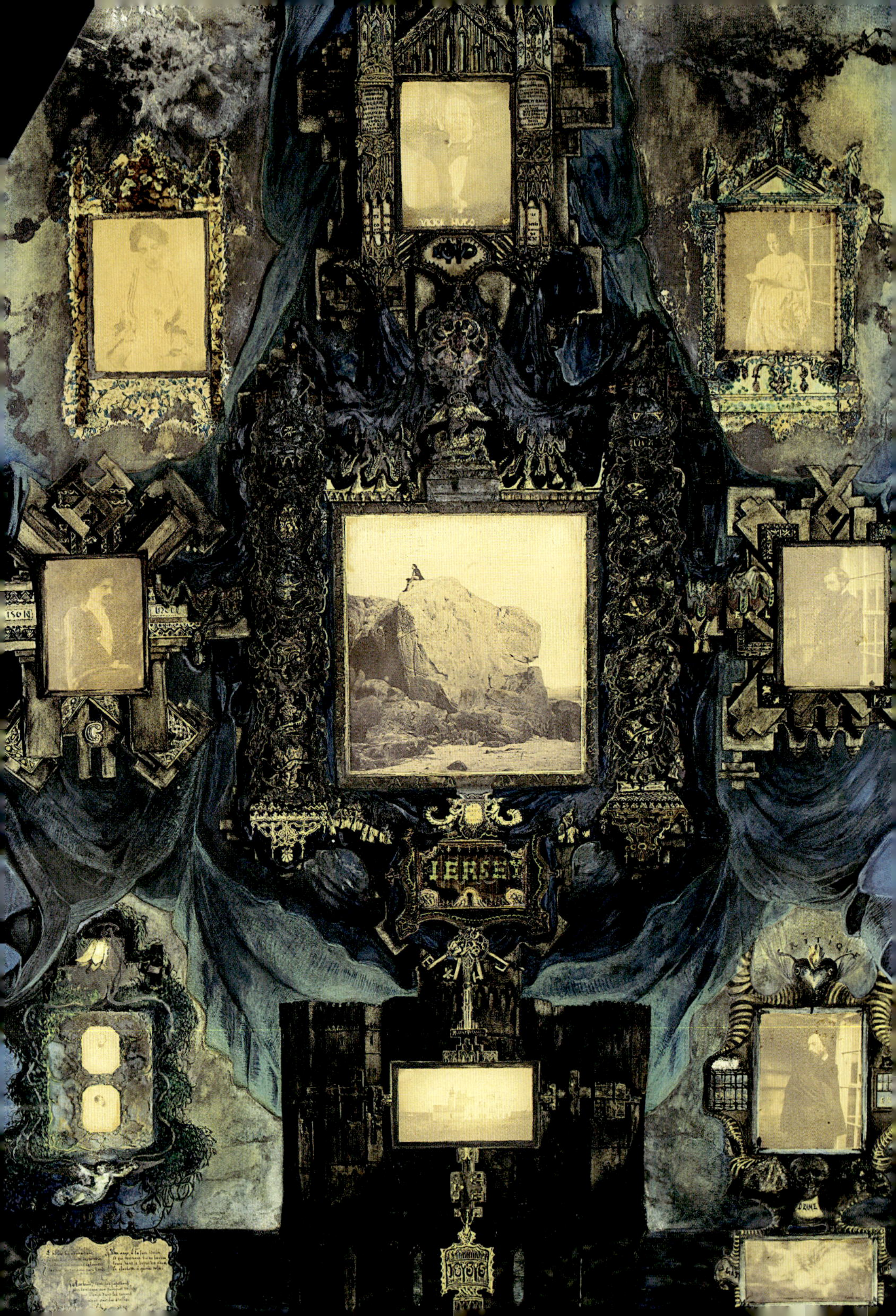
VICTOR HUGO
JERSEY

Victor Hugo and the Channel Islands

When he arrived on Jersey with Juliette Drouet and his son Charles on 5 August 1852, Victor Hugo was welcomed by his wife, his daughter Adèle and his faithful friend Auguste Vacquerie, who had arrived a few days earlier, and by some sixty fellow exiles.

'I thank you for your fraternal welcome,' he announced to them, 'which I fondly compare to the farewell our Belgian friends gave us. I left France on the quayside at Antwerp, I am returning to it here on the pier at Saint-Hélier.'[1]

The day after Louis-Napoléon Bonaparte's coup d'état, Victor Hugo had to flee Paris for his life with a passport procured by Juliette Drouet and arrived in Brussels on 12 December 1851. When in May 1852 he stopped work on *The History of a Crime* to write *Napoleon the Little*, he already knew that he would be gone from Belgium before the pamphlet's publication.

He wrote to his wife on 19 April 1852: 'As soon as I have sold my book I will go to London and from there to Jersey straight away. Jersey is a delightful English island seventeen leagues from the French coast. French is spoken there and one lives well and cheaply. All the exiles say that life there is wonderful. I will endeavour to find and probably will find an apartment for us on Jersey, perhaps a small house with a sea view and windows facing south, and maybe even a garden. […]. French is spoken on Jersey, which is invaluable because none of us speak English.' His second exile would thus be Jersey. Madame Hugo and her daughter arrived on the island on 31 July. The same day, Adèle wrote in her *Journal*: 'We have landed on Jersey […]. Saint-Hélier is a well-situated and clean town […]. We are staying at the Hôtel de la Pomme d'Or.' She wrote later: 'The island

ill. 5
Charles Hugo
(1826–71)
Collage, 1855–56
Photographs mounted on paper, watercoloured and inked
88 x 61 cm
MVHP-PH-3148

1. Victor Hugo, *Actes et paroles*, II, *Pendant l'exil*, 'En arrivant à Jersey'.

of Jersey is exquisitely and uniquely beautiful, a blooming garden bathed by the sea, a bouquet soaked in ocean spray with the scent of roses and the bitterness of the waves.'[2]

On 16 August, having probably hesitated between Saint-Aubin, Saint-Hélier and Gorey, the Hugo family finally moved into a large white house belonging to a shipowner, Mr Rose, in Marine Terrace, opposite Grève d'Azette and not far from the capital. In Adèle's *Journal*, there are accounts of the family's discovery of the island, of the excursions of an exile moved by its ocean views and megaliths steeped in mystery, and his relations with the many other French and foreign exiles who had found refuge in this 'free land'.

But Victor Hugo spent much of his time between 22 October 1852 and 9 October 1853 writing ninety of the hundred poems he included in *The Empire in the Pillory*. The collection was published in Brussels on 21 November 1853, to the great displeasure of Napoleon III, who had Hugo watched by Laurent, France's consular agent on the island. *Contemplations*, published in April 1856, also owes much to Jersey. Victor Hugo wrote more than a hundred of its poems there, as well as several score more for *The Fateful Years*, *The Year of Horrors*, *The Art of Being a Grandfather*, *Last Gleanings*, *The End of Satan*, *The Legend of the Ages*, *The Four Winds of the Spirit*, *Ocean* and *The Whole Lyre*. In short, he found inspiration there.

It was also an island of discoveries. On his return from a trip to Caen, where he had met the photographer Edmond Bacot, his son Charles initiated Auguste Vacquerie to the Daguerreotype. Victor Hugo himself occasionally played a direct hand in the staging of their photographs of the family, friends and entourage, Marine Terrace and the island. This gave rise to a project, announced in *La Lumière* on 6 and 8 October 1853: 'Jersey and the Channel Islands, verses by Victor Hugo; prose by Auguste Vacquerie, Charles Hugo and François-Victor Hugo; photographs by Charles Hugo; drawings by Victor Hugo.' But all that remains of the project are the photographs (Mont Orgueil Castle, the exile at the summit of the 'Rocher des Proscrits' ['Exiles' Rock'], the ruins of Grosnez Castle, Grève d'Azette, etc.) and the text Victor Hugo wrote for this collective publication, much of which he included in *The Archipelago of the Channel*, the prelude to *The Toilers of the Sea*.

The arrival of Victor Hugo's friend Delphine de Girardin on Jersey on 6 September 1853 prompted his discovery of another novel prac-

2. Adèle Hugo, *Journal*, 6 August 1852, Maison de Victor Hugo, Paris, MVHP-ms-α8888.

tice also much in vogue in Paris, table-turning. Initially sceptical, he began taking this means of communicating with voices in the ether seriously at a séance during which his daughter Léopoldine made her presence felt. Gathered around a small tripod table placed on the dining room table at Marine Terrace, they spoke with Marat, Chénier, Shakespeare, Androcles' lion, Galileo, Joan of Arc, Diderot and others. 'The table-turning phenomenon,' he wrote to François-Victor, 'does not diminish the 19th century but greatens it. The table-turning phenomenon does not hinder human liberty and gives wings to human faith.'[3]

These spiritist adventures 'at the very tip of the headland of dreams', these encounters with the 'intermediary world' and the beyond, soon made themselves felt in Hugo's work.

But they did not distract the fierce opponent of the coup d'état from his political commitment and the other causes he so nobly defended. It was from Jersey that he intervened to prevent the murderer Tapner, imprisoned on Guernsey, from being hanged. 'It is up to you,' he wrote to the inhabitants of the neighbouring island, 'to abolish the death penalty on Guernsey; it is up to you to save a man from "hanging until he is dead" on the 27th of January; it is up to you to prevent this terrible spectacle from leaving a black mark in your beautiful sky.'[4]

It was from Jersey that he addressed his fellow exiles from Poland, hailing 'the blessed dawn of the United States of Europe. Oh! What a marvellous realisation it will be! No more borders, no more customs, no more wars, no more weapons, no more armies, no more proletariat, no more ignorance, no more misery.'[5]

It was again from Jersey that he spoke out against the war waged in the Crimea by France, Britain and Turkey against the Russians, who had attacked the Ottoman Empire. 'In the present hour, by the thousand, soon by the hundred thousand, the French, English, Turks and Russians will be slitting each other's throats in the Orient in front of a heap of ruins.'[6]

On 10 October 1855, the newspaper *L'Homme* published Félix Pyat's 'Letter to the Queen', which Victor Hugo privately described as a 'huge blunder', but whose editors, forced to leave Jersey, he publicly supported. On 27 October, the Constable of St Clement

3. *Ibid*, 27 April 1854.
4. Victor Hugo, *Actes et paroles*, II, *Pendant l'exil*, 'Aux habitants de Guernesey'.
5. *Ibid*, 'Vingt-troisième anniversaire de la révolution polonaise'.
6. *Ibid*, 'La Guerre d'Orient'.

informed him that he in turn had been served with an the expulsion order.
He had arrived on the island with Charles; he left with François-Victor and Juliette Drouet on the 31st, noting in his diary: 'Left Jersey at 7 h 1/4 in the morning, arrived Guernsey at 10, heavy sea, rain, squalls. Jersey, rock, then cloud then shadow then nothing. Difficult landing. Enormous waves. Small boats overloaded with men and luggage.'
They landed only a few metres from the Hôtel de l'Europe (now Woolworths), where Victor Hugo and his son stayed, while Juliette and her maid took rooms at the Crown Hotel (now the Ship and Crown Hotel) on the same quayside.
On 1 November, he reassured his wife: 'The reception was good; crowd on the quayside; silence, but sympathy, at least apparently; everyone took off their hats when I passed. I am writing to you with a wonderful view before my eyes. Even in the rain and fog, the arrival on Guernsey is splendid.'
He dated the final poem of *Contemplations*, 'To the One Who Stayed in France':
'2 November 1855, day of our dead':

'Since it is at present impossible for me to throw
Even a sprig of heather on her mute grave
She can at least have my soul
Oh, black wind whose steps I hear on my ceiling!
Storm, winter, beating my panes with your hail!
Seas, nights! If I put it in this book it was for her!'

The very same day, a few hours before Charles arrived, he found a house at 20 Hauteville Street that had been empty for some time. He later found out that it was said to be haunted, and that the previous tenant, a pastor, had left due to the noises at night. He signed a lease immediately and rented a few pieces of furniture.
The exiled poet and Juliette Drouet bought the house, initially called Hauteville Terrace, then Hauteville House, in April 1864. Juliette lived there from then on. It was also known as 'Hauteville Féerie' or 'Fairy'. Some of the furniture in the drawing room and Juliette's bedroom was installed in a room in La Maison de Victor Hugo in place des Vosges in Paris.
The present owners of the house, now called La Vigie, have placed a plaque by the front door: 'Hauteville Fairy – First house of Victor Hugo, from 1855 to 1856, and Juliette Drouet's home from 1864.'

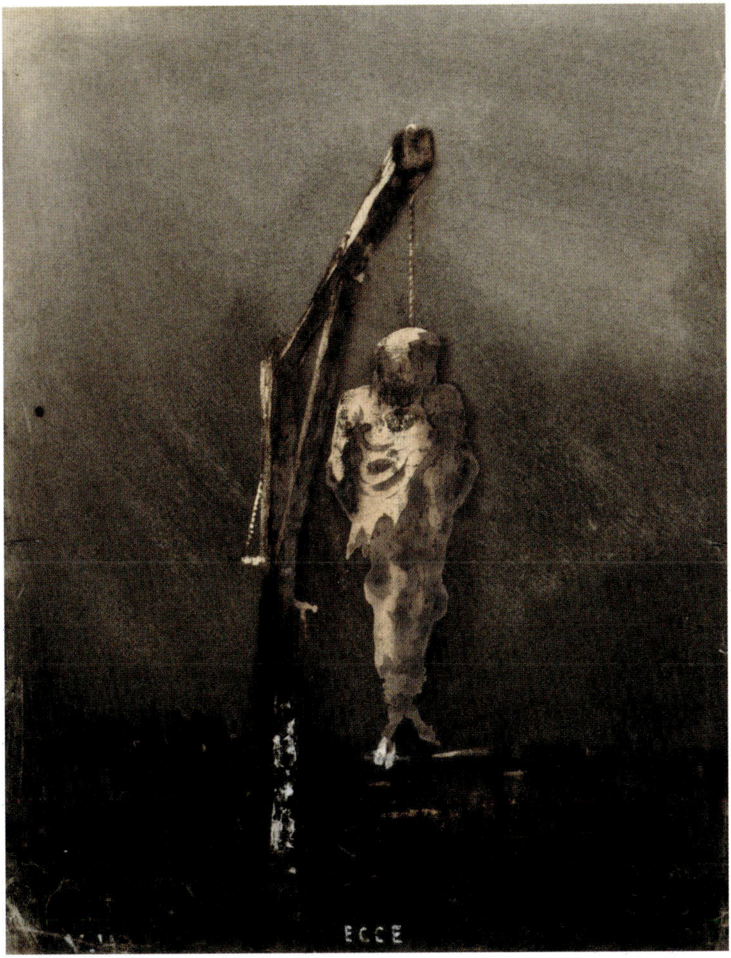

ill. 6
Victor Hugo
(1802–85)
"Ecce", 1854
Pen and brush, brown ink and ink wash, black ink wash, charcoal, highlights of white gouache, reserves on beige paper
50.8 x 34.9 cm
MVHP-D-124

In the afternoon on 7 November, Victor Hugo and Juliette Drouet went on a tour of the island in a carriage: 'Granite in the southern part, sand in the northern part,' he wrote in *The Archipelago of the Channel*, 'here steep slopes, there the downs; an inclined plane of meadows with rolling hills, relieved by rocks; for a fringe to this carpet of green wrinkled in folds, the foam of the ocean.'[7]
Mme Hugo and her daughter Adèle arrived on Guernsey two days later and the entire family moved into Hauteville. 'From our windows we can see all the Channel Islands and the port below; the view is splendid,' Mme Hugo wrote to Mme Paul Meurice.[8]

7. 'Guernsey' (chapter III).
8. Letter, 25 November 1855, in Jean Massin (ed.), *Victor Hugo, Œuvres complètes* (Paris, Club français du livre, 1967–70) vol. X, p. 1220.

Victor Hugo spent most of his time reading the proofs of *Contemplations*. On 23 April 1856, when the collection of poems was put on sale in Paris, it was, in Paul Meurice's words, 'a stunning success': the Pagnerre bookshop sold 1,000 copies on the first day and Michel Lévy some 1,300. Victor Hugo's publisher, Hetzel, arrived on Guernsey on 1 May and it was decided to publish a second edition. Victor Hugo did his arithmetic: for the first time in his life he could own a house.

The *Gazette de Guernesey* informed its readers in its 24 May number: 'Monsieur Victor Hugo has just bought a house at Hauteville. We are delighted. It is proof that the great poet feels at home with us and intends to stay on Guernsey.' He had bought no. 38 Hauteville Street, a hundred metres further up the street than his previous lodgings, and baptised it Liberty House before opting for Hauteville House. He confided to Jules Janin two months later: 'Do you realise that at the moment I am building almost a house; no longer having a homeland, I want to have a roof [...]. The house on Guernsey, its three floors, its roof, its garden, its front steps, its crypt, its henhouse, its lookout and its platform, everything comes entirely from *Contemplations*. *Contemplations* will pay for everything, from the first beam to the last tile. This book has given me a roof.'[9]

Mme Hugo was only too right when she wrote to Paul Meurice's wife: 'My husband will come to life here. He will fix up his house according to his taste, furnish it like his lodgings in Paris. It will have nothing of the country house about it, of one of those houses that are accidents, so modest that they are unpretentious and leave one free. Into this one my husband is putting his gildings, his wall hangings, all his fantasy and all his care. Here we are again hanging on the walls.'[10]

Victor Hugo spent his first night at Hauteville House on 5 November, and Juliette Drouet, who stayed for a few months in lodgings at 8 Havelet Street, moved into a house closer to Hauteville House, La Fallue (now an annexe of the Pandora Hotel). 'I now have my lookout, thanks to you, my ineffably good little man,' she wrote to him on 2 July 1856. 'I will be able to see you at nearly every time of day.'[11]

The first two Guernsey diaries (1856 and 1857) tell us much about how Victor Hugo furnished Hauteville House. Constantly on the

9. Letter, 16 August 1856, *ibid.*, p. 1263.
10. Letter, 17 October 1856, *ibid.*, p. 1264.
11. Paris, BNF, NAF, f° 16377.

lookout for curios, pieces of old junk and objects of value, according to Juliette Drouet, he carried out 'raids on all the junkshops' on the island. Everything was piled up until it found a place here or there: 'Hindu paintings', 'Saxony soup tureen and dishes', 'Turkish carpet', 'long Chinese mirror with a lacquer border', 'Florentine wardrobe', 'Brussels carpet', 'antiquities from Peru', 'Japanese ornament'.

If the privateer who had built the house in the early 19th century had returned, he might well have thought that Victor Hugo, like himself, was involved in some sort of trafficking…

Before the entry 'old chest hunt' first appeared in the exile's diaries, aided by his son Charles and more frequently by Juliette Drouet, he bought chests of all kinds, 'with gothic panels', 'with diamonds', 'with arabesques', 'with chimera', 'with figures', 'with scrollwork', 'with apostles', and in every style: gothic, 15th century, Charles VIII, Renaissance, Louis XIII, etc. In a few months he had acquired sixty, which he then reused for other purposes in most of the rooms in the house.

Gradually – Victor Hugo regretted the 'tremendous slowness' if his craftsmen – the house was transformed: the first dinner in the dining room was held on 14 May 1957, and the studio was ready on 16 September of the same year; the tapestries room and the antechamber were finished on 5 May 1858. The last major undertaking, in autumn 1861, was the construction of the 'glazed roof room' on the third floor, known as the 'lookout'. Victor Hugo inaugurated it on 29 December by reading a letter from Juliette Drouet.

It was here in this room, freezing cold in winter, boiling hot in summer, looking out over the ocean, that he finished or wrote many of his works, including *The Legend of the Ages*, *Les Misérables*, *William Shakespeare*, *Songs of the Street and Wood*, *The Toilers of the Sea*, *The Man Who Laughs* and *Torquemada*.

He expressed his gratitude to the island of Guernsey in the dedication of his novel *The Toilers of the Sea*, which owes everything to his close relationship with the ocean: 'I dedicate this book to the rock of hospitality and liberty, to that nook of ancient Norman soil where dwells the noble little race of the sea, to the island of Guernsey, severe yet gentle, my present asylum, probably my tomb.'

Victor Hugo continued his indefatigable struggle for all kinds of liberties: his interventions in support of John Brown, the slavery abolitionist sentenced to death in the United States, the Mexican people attacked by French troops, the uprising in Cuba against the island's Spanish rulers and the people of Crete oppressed by the Turks.

ill. 7
Jean-Marie Boucher
(1870–1939)
Victor Hugo, 1802–1885, 1906–1913
Sculpture, stone
Dedication to *The Toilers of the Sea* inscribed on the plinth: 'To the rock of hospitality and liberty/ to that nook of ancient Norman soil / where dwells the noble little race of the sea /
To the isle of Guernsey severe yet gentle...
V.H.'
Candie Gardens, Saint-Peter's Port, Guernsey

From 10 March 1862, the crusade against misery he had waged for so long found new expression in a gesture that was not merely symbolic, he invited the poor children of the island to dinner. He explained to Octave Lacroix on 30 June 1862: 'Every Tuesday, I give a dinner for fifteen poor children, chosen among the island's most destitute, and my family and I serve them; in doing so I try to make equality and fraternity understood in this feudal land.'[12]

His wife and Charles made frequent trips to Paris and Brussels. His daughter Adèle, madly in love with Lieutenant Pinson, whom she met on Jersey, left Guernsey for good in 1863, for Halifax then Barbados. François-Victor returned to Paris in January 1865 after the death of his fiancée, Emily de Putron.

Only the faithful and discreet Juliette Drouet remained constantly at his side, sharing the hardships of exile with her beloved poet. On 15 August 1870, she went with him to Brussels, and on 5 September, the day after the fall of the Second Empire, a triumphant welcome was given to the man who in August 1859 had refused the decree of amnesty, writing: 'Faithful to the vow I made with my conscience, I will share exile and liberty to the very end. When freedom returns I will return.'[13]

The two lovers returned to Hauteville House three times, for twelve months in 1872–73, for a week in 1875 and for four months in 1878.

Gérard Pouchain

12. Victor Hugo, *Œuvres complètes*, *op. cit.*, t. XII, p. 1184.
13. Victor Hugo, *Actes et paroles*, II, *Pendant l'exil*, 'L'Amnistie'.

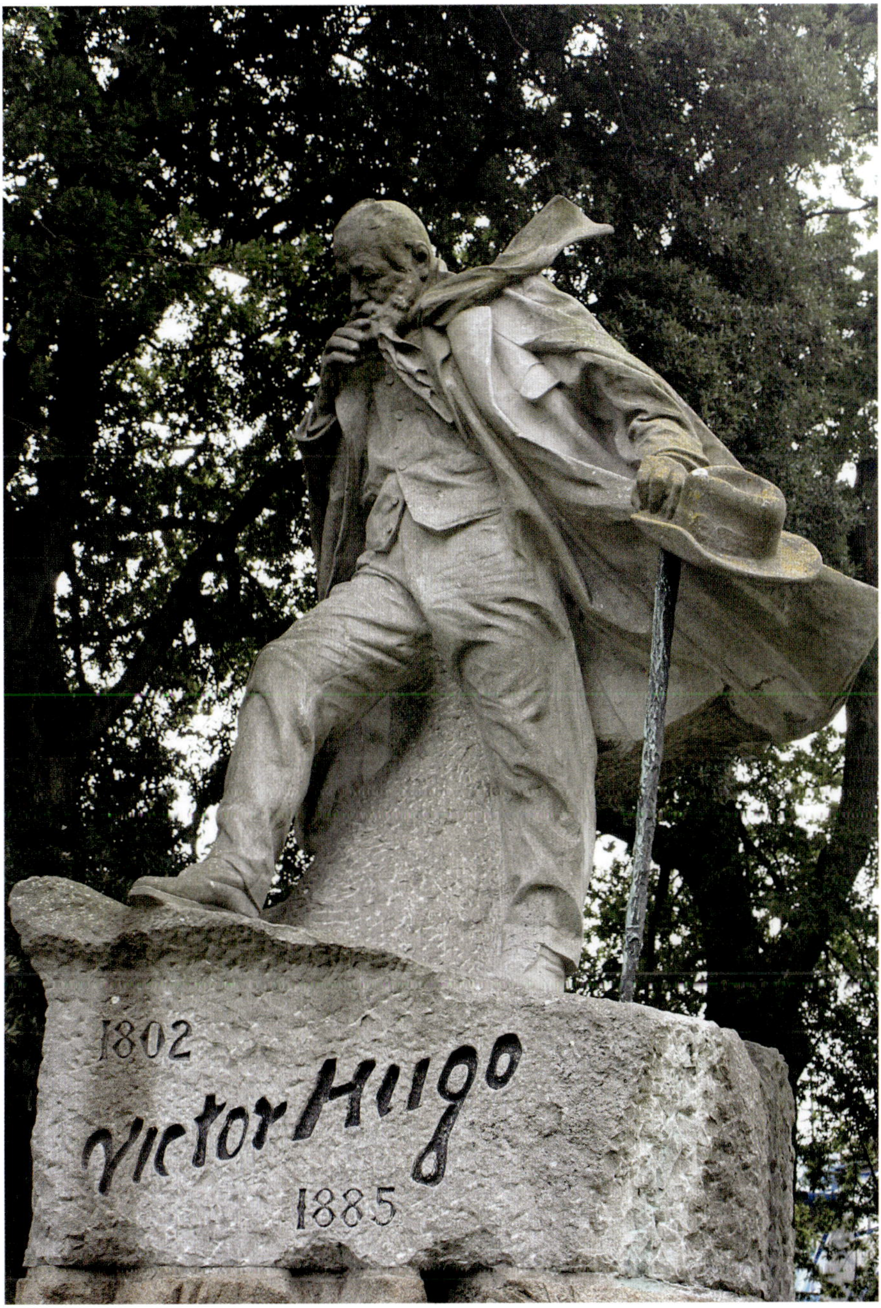
1802
Victor Hugo
1885

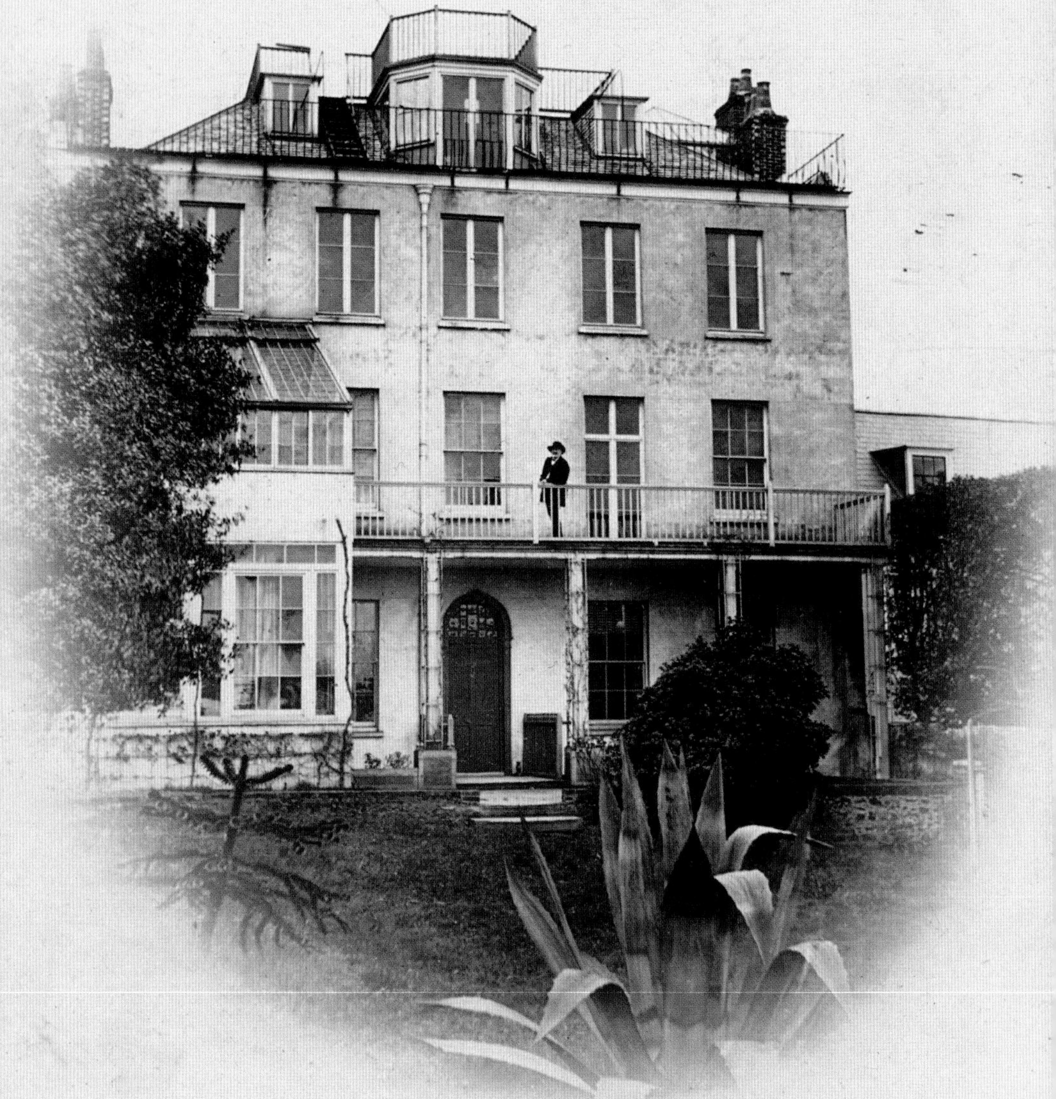

Hauteville House

'I'm going to fix up the house. […] It will be the trilogy of builders, painters and upholsterers. After which, the doors will be thrown wide open on the French side, upon poetry and good and valiant hearts […].'

Victor Hugo to Paul Meurice, 15 June 1856

ill. 8
Arsène Garnier
(1822–1900)
Victor Hugo on the first-floor balcony at Hauteville House
Albumen print
16.8 x 12.5 cm
MVHP-PH-3713

Comprised essentially of a three-man team of craftsmen, Tom Gor, Jean and James, with the carpenter Mauger and then his son as foreman, this 'trilogy' worked at Hauteville House for several years. Although most of the work was completed in 1859, more went on until 1862. To fit out his residence, Victor Hugo 'turned himself into an interior designer and decorator, upholsterer, sculptor, cabinet-maker, builder and architect,'[1] transforming Hauteville House into a veritable work of art à la Hugo, whose creation one can follow day by day in his diaries.[2]

1. René Weiss, *La Maison de Victor Hugo à Guernesey (Hauteville House), propriété de la Ville de Paris* (Paris, Imprimerie nationale) 1928, p. 22.
2. These diaries are now in the Bibliothèque nationale de France, Paris.

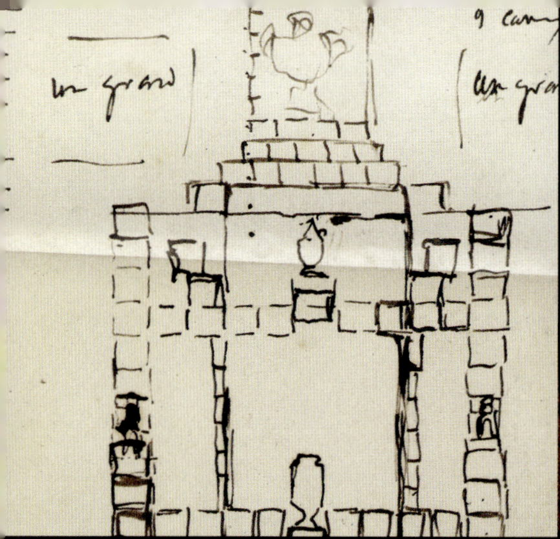
un grand

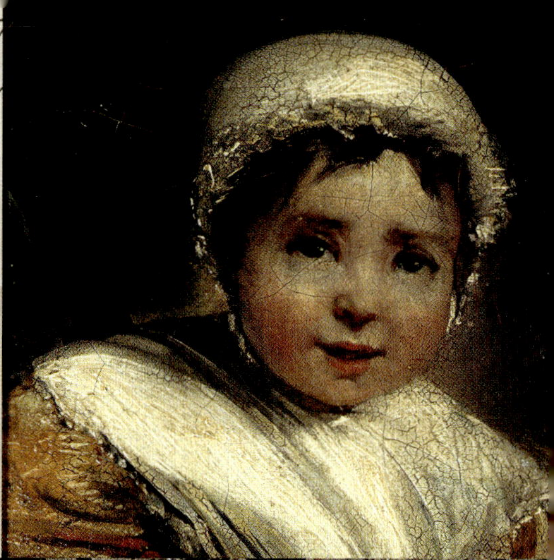

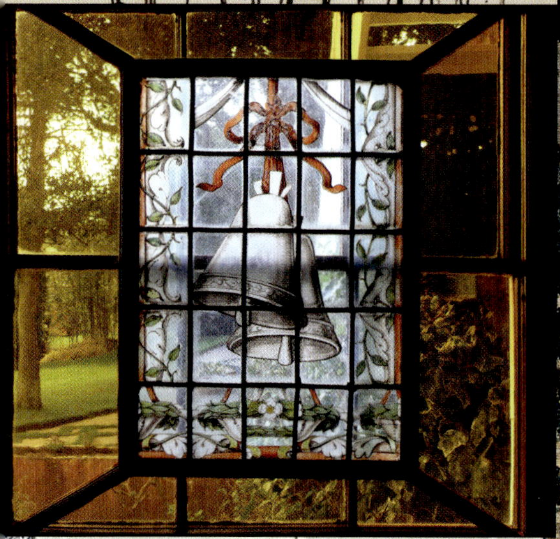

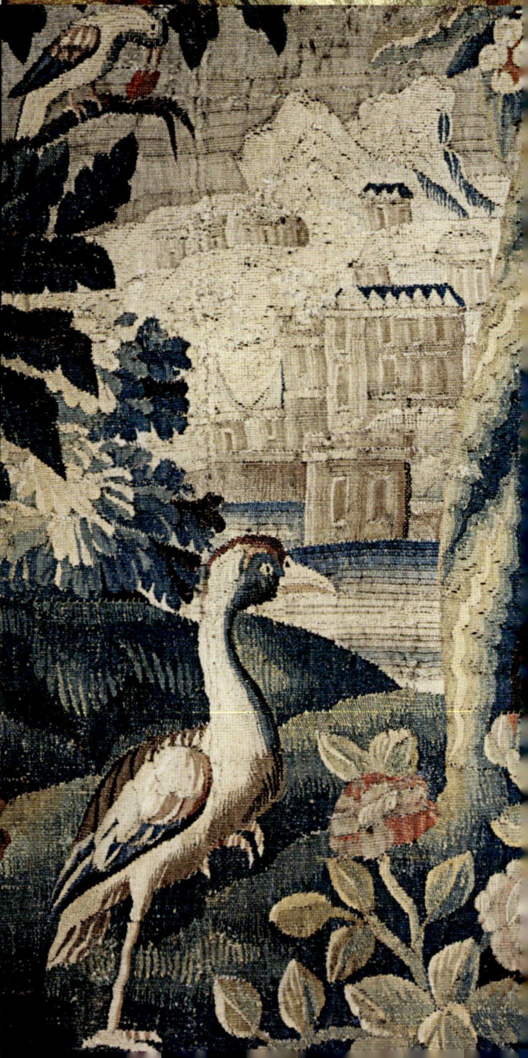

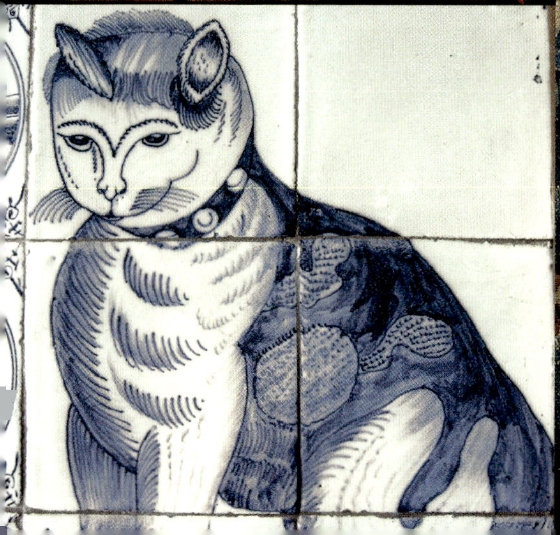

Ground floor

The hall and waiting room

As in a medieval church, as soon as one crosses the threshold of Hauteville House one is immediately plunged into a solemn, mysterious atmosphere that can instil 'a kind of shudder and a vague sense of divinity'.[3] In the half-darkness, unaware of what awaits one in this residence gradually revealing itself, one is welcomed by a Gothic-inspired wooden portal, above which bottle-bottom panes in the Flemish and Dutch manner filter the light from outside. Signed and titled *VICTOR HUGO NOSTRE-DAME DE PARIS* in the middle of the entablature, it announces the parallelism between writing and architecture present throughout the house, and is quite literally 'Hauteville House's frontispiece'.[4] Based on a cathedral portal, it is surmounted by a glazed triptych and divided into two by a Corinthian column, each side surmounted by medallion portraits of Victor Hugo and his daughter Adèle by David d'Angers. The sculpted pediment above the middle section of the glass triptych, evoking a mask with huge, gaping eye sockets, is reminiscent of Gaudi's anthropomorphic creations half a century later.

On 25 January 1859 Victor Hugo inscribed *AMA. CREDE* on the other side of the portal. He explained these words in a letter to Juliette Drouet on 16 February (date of their anniversary) 1859: 'Oh! that our spirit should always return to this: believe; and our heart always to this: love. *Love – Believe.* This is what I wrote above

3. François-René de Chateaubriand, *Génie du christianisme*, 1802.
4. Charles Hugo, *Chez Victor Hugo par un passant*, preface by A. Lecanu, with twelve etchings by Maxime Lalanne (Paris, Cadart et Luquet, 1864) p. 27.

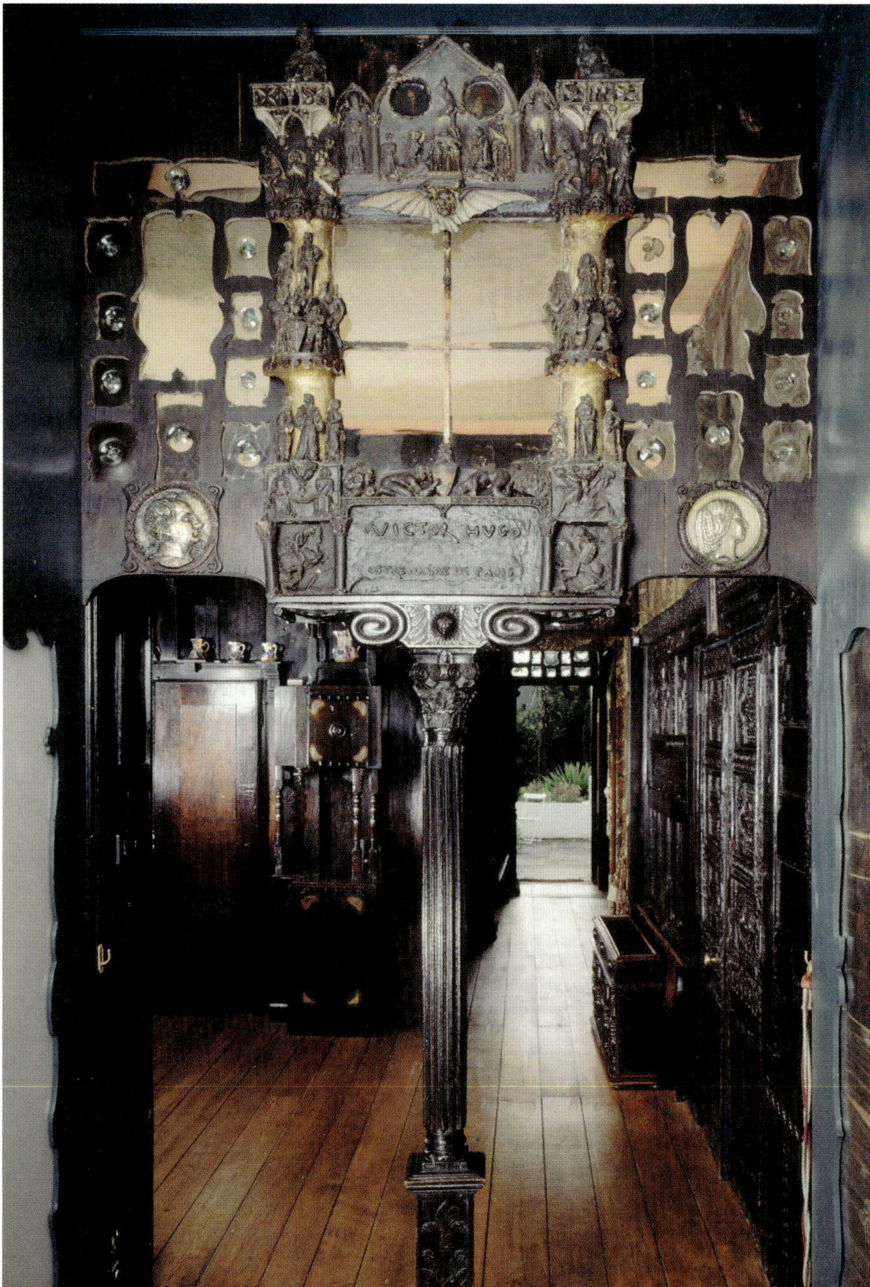
VICTOR HUGO

the door to my house. I am also writing it on the door to my heart, which opens onto love, and on the door of your heart, which opens onto heaven.' *Ama, Crede* became the title of a series of poems in *Songs of the Street and the Wood*, written on Guernsey and published in 1865.

ill. 9
Hauteville House, the 'Nostre-Dame' portal in the hall

Neo-Gothic Style

Although styles of different periods and geographical origins mingle in the hall, it is neo-Gothic which dominates. It had been the huge success of Victor Hugo's *Notre-Dame de Paris* (1831, 1st complete edition 1832) that had sparked the French craze for all things Gothic in the 1830s.
In 1825, he became aware of the dilapidated state of France's medieval heritage on a trip to the Alps with Charles Nodier. From 1835 to 1848 he took part in the successive 'Arts and Monuments' committees charged with drawing up an inventory of French monuments in order to organise their protection against vandalism. With Prosper Mérimée, he supported the architect Jean-Baptiste Lassus, who restored the church of Saint-Germain-l'Auxerrois, and the Sainte-Chapelle and Notre-Dame with Eugène Viollet-le-Duc. But it was above all via his writing that Victor Hugo succeeded in raising public awareness of the state of France's medieval heritage. He committed himself to the defence of the 'admirable monuments of the Middle Ages' in his 'Note on the destruction of the monuments of France' (published in 1831), and spoke out against 'the demolition of the France of old' in 'Beware of the demolishers!' (1832). The success of *Notre-Dame de Paris* greatly aided these two articles 'by an amateur antique dealer'.[5]
Before his exile, particularly on his summer holidays with Juliette Drouet, he visited gothic châteaux, abbeys, churches and cathedrals, sketching their architectural details in his notebooks. From 1838 to 1840, he discovered the great gothic cathedrals of Strasbourg, Cologne and Aachen, and the medievals castles of the Rhineland, which inspired many drawings and the book *The Rhine* (1842).
The *Nostre-Dame* portal is a reminder of this Parisian literary past and his travels before exile, but also a contemporary decor for some of the poems devoted to Christian history in the first part of *The Legend of the Ages*, in which the writer brings the Late Middle Ages back to life in 'The Knights-Errant', 'The Little King of Galicia' and 'Eviradnus'.

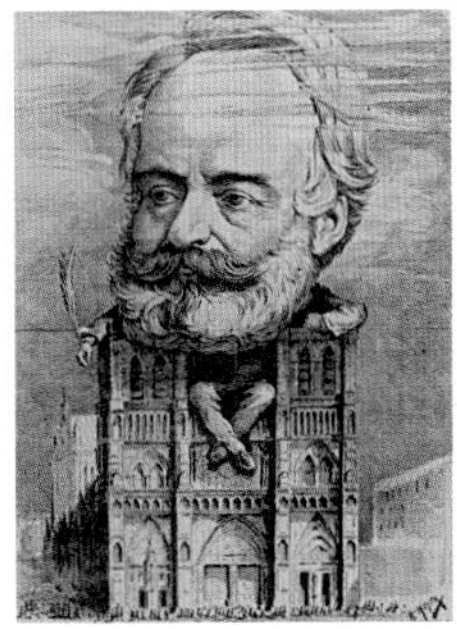

Henri Meyer
(1844–99)
Victor Hugo, The Giant,
1st year, no. 10, Sunday
26 April 1868
64 x 48.5 cm
MVHP-E-3072

5. Jean Gaudon, 'Éloge du décor', in Roland Recht (ed.) *Victor Hugo et le débat patrimonial* (Paris, INP/Somogy, 2003) p. 92.

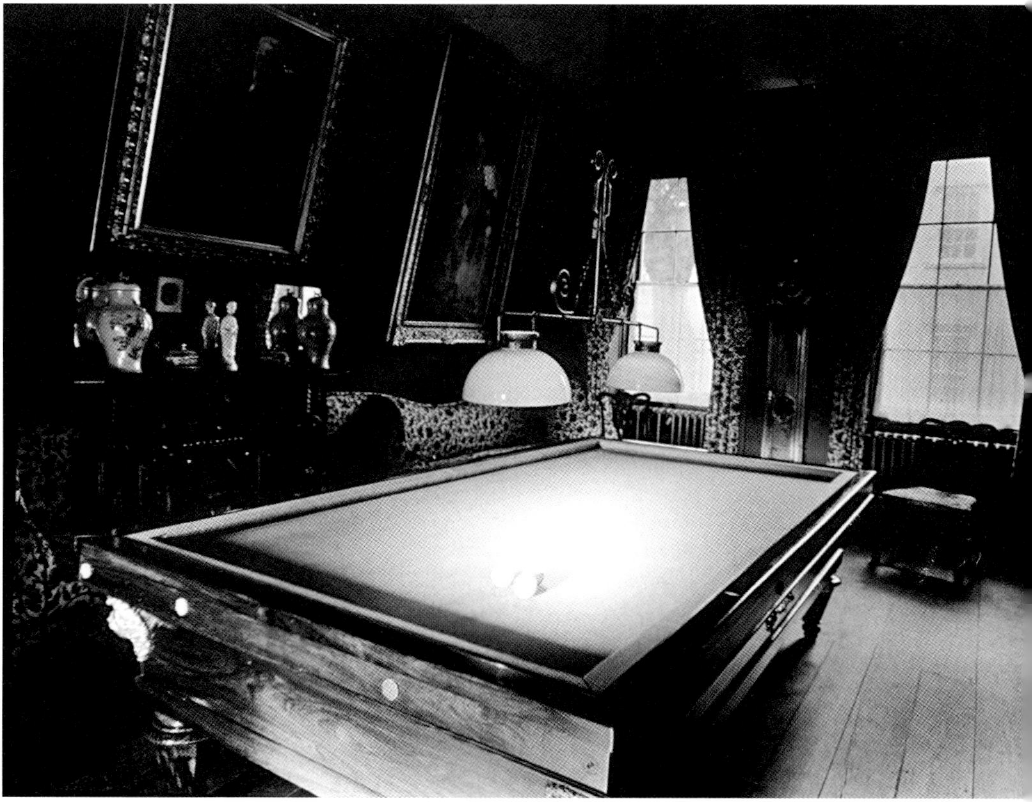

ill. 10
Olivier Mériel
(born 1955)
Hauteville, billiard room, Tuesday 10 February 1998, 10 a.m.
Contact print
30 x 39.5 cm
MVHP-PH-2010-6-1

The billiard room

'Hauteville House has remained rather like the "house of souls" for us, because everything there speaks of the dear departed.'

Georges Hugo, *My Grandfather*, Paris, Calmann-Lévy, 1902, p. 34.

Beyond the *Nostre-Dame* portal, on the left, the hall gives onto the former bedroom of Auguste Vacquerie, converted into a waiting room, and to the right onto the billiard room. As one goes through the door into the billiard room, one passes beneath the word *AVE*, carved in the woodwork beneath a Madonna and Child.
The billiard table was bought for 995 francs and delivered on 10 February 1857. Victor Hugo placed it in the middle of the room, which was finished in 1858. Sheila Gaudon recalled that 'the installation of a billiard table only concretised the isolation. The father, that "gentle tyrant" – François-Victor's expression – refused to understand that it was more fun playing in a "billiard hall", where one could smoke and drink with friends[...], than at home.'[6] And indeed there is nothing playful or convivial at all about his room, which is more like a private sanctuary dedicated to a family's memories.

The billiard room is a veritable family portrait gallery, in which descendants have replaced the traditional gallery of ancestors in aristocratic homes, the only ancestor present here being Léopold Hugo, Victor's father. The large oil paintings by Louis Boulanger, of Léopoldine at four years old (1828), Victor (1833), Adèle Hugo (1839) and *Adèle with a Cherry*, hang next to the portrait of Léopoldine as a baby by Julie Duvidal de Montferrier, those of the writer and his son François-Victor by Auguste de Châtillon (1836) and François-Victor by Charles de Champmartin (1834). Two works by Champmartin evoke happy memories of the eldest daughter who died so young: *Léopoldine's First Communion* and *Léopoldine with the Book of Hours*. There is also a facsimile of a portrait drawing of Léopoldine by Dubufe. Victor Hugo referred to these images recalling the past in a letter to Louis Boulanger on 9 April 1866: 'In my dilapidated exile house I have constantly before me several power-

6.. Sheila Gaudon, 'M. Victor Marie Hugo, propriétaire à Guernesey', in *Exilium Vita Est. Victor Hugo à Guernesey*, exh. cat. (Paris, Paris-Musées, 2002) p. 22.

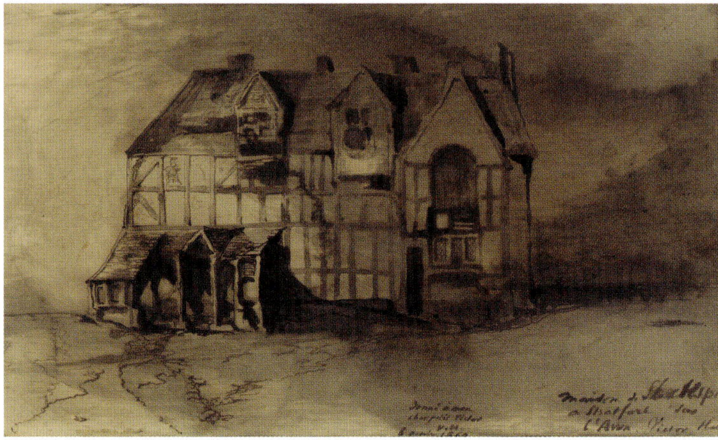

ill. 11
Victor Hugo
(1802–85)
Shakespeare's House at Stratford on Avon
Pen, feather brush and brown ink wash on paper
21.5 x 37.8 cm
Glued by Victor Hugo to card bearing traces of the same wash as the drawing,
34.1 x 48.7 cm
In the middle in brown ink: 'donné à mon/ cher petit Victor/ V.H./ 8 octobre 1860' ['given to my dear little Victor, 8 October 1860']
MVHP-D-958

ful and brilliant works signed by Louis Boulanger. I look at them and wonder: Where are the roses of yesteryear? – You are still my beloved painter friend, my sorely missed companion, one of those two brothers at the beginning, at once even more precious and dearer.' When his descendants donated Hauteville House to the City of Paris in 1927, they commissioned Eugénie Venot d'Auteroche to paint copies of the Boulanger and Châtillon portraits. The originals were returned to the Maison de Victor Hugo in Paris, where they hung when the Hugo family lived there from 1832 to 1848.

All these portraits hung alongside the drawings Victor Hugo entitled *Souvenirs*, and progressively displayed in the billiard room: *Souvenirs of Spain*, *Switzerland* and *the Black Forest* and *Shakespeare's House at Stratford Upon Avon*, *Old House*, *Burg in Ruins*, *The Snake Fountain*, *The Hanged Man* and *Justitia*. In the autumn of 1859, Victor Hugo had these drawings framed. For conservation reasons, the originals were replaced by facsimiles in 1997.
The *Souvenirs* brought back memories of an idealised past, particularly his annual trips with Juliette Drouet, who took a discreet part in the life of the family she had frequented so closely during exile. Chantal Brière has shown how the fireplace in the middle of the room is packed with allusions to Juliette,[7] Victor's 'angel adored' or 'sweet angel': the fireplace is decorated with a winged angel's head and surmounted by the date *1653*, which can be deciphered as

7. Chantal Brière, *Victor Hugo et le roman architectural* (Paris, Honoré Champion, 2007) p. 506.

follows: 16 for the 16h of February, date of the anniversary of their love; 5 for the month of Juliette's birthday; and 3 for the year they met, 1833. The gilt bronze grotesques on the corners of the billiard table echo the angel's head.
In January 1866, Victor Hugo had the room padlocked then filled it with some forty packing cases still full of objects. He noted in his dairy on 16 May 1866: 'In the billiard room I have stored all the objects that were in the studio. The billiard room will be closed and padlocked, and the studio and tapestries room will remain in free use.'
The billiard room became a cenotaph, with the small Egyptian statuette above the clock in one of its corners acting as emblem of a space now given over to the worship of a lost past. Accompanying the souls of the deceased into the next world, it wards off time's implacable march towards death, of which we are constantly reminded by its noisy ticking.

The tapestries room

'The lower drawing room will be superb. It will even be one of the most beautiful. The ceiling is finished. Tapestry and panelling with sculpted oak cartouches. [...] There will be the hunt on the wall facing the fireplace, the fauna to the left of the door and another charming tapestry, which he cut out of one of those Auguste brought him.'

Charles Hugo to his mother, 18 February 1858[8]

A double door connects the billiard room and tapestries room, named after the 17th and 18th-century tapestries covering its walls and ceiling. In the warmer atmosphere of this room, the family sometimes took coffee and held small, intimate soirées.

The tapestries room is a veritable hymn to nature, with plant-inspired decoration present everywhere: the rosettes, foliation, palm leaves and acanthi sculpted in the panelling, the floral motifs of the large Aubusson tapestries and their borders, the red peonies in the tapestry on the wall on the studio side, the corolla-shaped pink glass ceiling lamps, the plant decoration of the oriental carpets,

8. Maison de Victor Hugo, Paris, MVHP ms α588.

the flowers and butterflies painted by Charles and Mme Hugo on the mirrors, the blue flowers on the faience soup tureen, etc. Even the plants in the garden seem to be present via their reflections in the mirrors. Nature is also represented by mythology, in the satyr motif on the fireplace and the large 'faun tapestry', hung on 27 February 1858, depicting an offering to Pan. The room also seems to echo some of the poems in *Songs of the Street and Wood*.

The tapestries room also gives onto a photographic darkroom, whose door is concealed by a hanging and a mirror painted by Charles Hugo. Having done a lot of photography on Jersey from 1853, Charles continued to practice this new art on Guernesey with Auguste Vacquerie, taking numerous collodion portraits of his father and his entourage and developing them in this darkroom, alluded to in the sixth poem of 'Old Age and Young Age Mixed Together', part six of *The Art of Being a Grandfather* (1876): 'Jeanne was on a dry bread diet in the small dark room.'

ill. 12
Hauteville House, the tapestries room

ill. 13
Olivier Mériel
(born 1955)
Hauteville, the tapestries room, Wednesday 11 February 1998, 10 a.m.
Contact print
28.7 x 37.5 cm
MVHP-PH-2671

The whole of the right-hand wall is taken up by a monumental composition in wood, largely composed of reused chest panels, into which Victor Hugo inset the Delft faience fireplace. François-Victor wrote to his mother on 9 March 1858: 'The fireplace in the new drawing room will be a monument. What's more, this room will be excellent and splendid, comfortable and indestructible. This is what true rooms are made of: tapestries and oak.'[9] Charles also showered praise on this fireplace in a letter to Adèle Hugo on 14 March 1858: 'The fireplace is finished. It is a veritable cathedral. [...] I forgot to say that the fireplace manages to be beautiful and handy, and that one can light a fire in it, a commendable thing in a fireplace designed by papa.'[10]
Partitioned like a triptych or the nave and side-aisles of a church, this composition brings together geniuses cited by Victor Hugo in *William Shakespeare* (1864). The statues of Saint Paul holding a book (*ad libro*) and Saint John gazing heavenward (*ad coelum*), echo one another on either side of the four columns supporting the central coffer. Other great names are celebrated in the lower part of the composition: *Moses*, *Socrates*, *Christ*, *Columbus*, *Luther* and *Washington* carved on the right-hand volute; and on the left, *Job*, *Isaiah*, *Homer*, *Aeschylus*, *Dante*

9. MVHP ms α312.
10. MVHP ms α590.

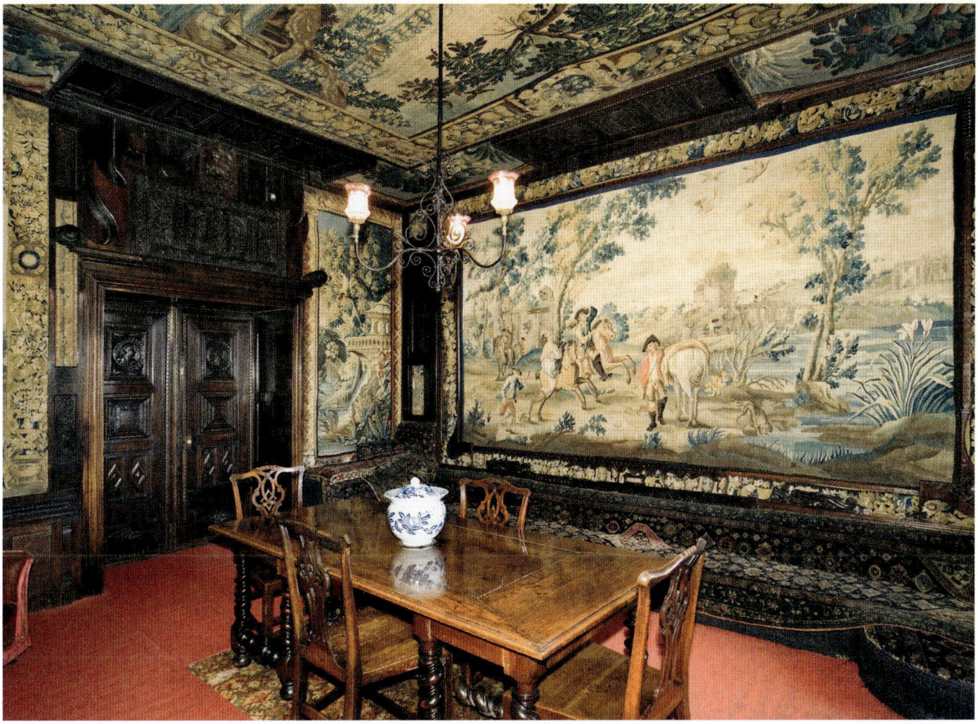

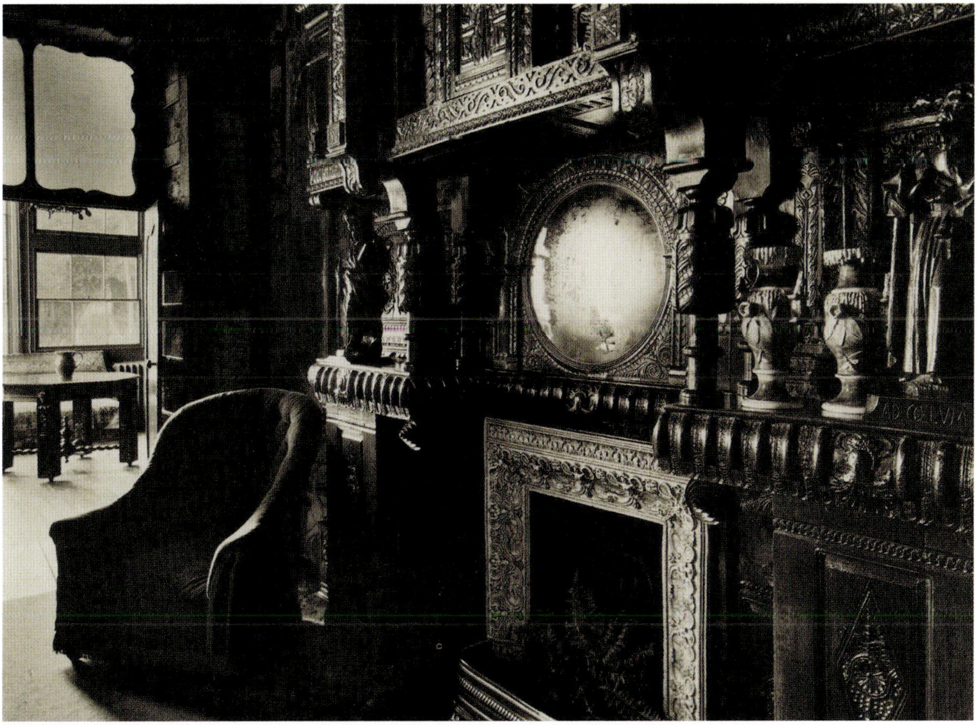

and *Shakespeare*, who 'close the two first doors of barbarism, the antique door and the gothic door' (preface to *Cromwell*), and finally *Molière*. Some of them are 'equals', geniuses in whom 'human thought attains [...] its full intensity' (*William Shakespeare*). Victor Hugo's composition, an 'architectural figuration of enumeration',[11] is a spatial concretisation associating genius and architecture.

The room is reflected in the convex mirror at the heart of this 'monument', whose reflective power evokes a photographic lens but also embodies artistic creation, the finished work that condenses the infinite, the genius's visionary eye. Unlike the two-dimensional mirror, which reflects only a 'lifeless image with no relief', the convex mirror is a metaphor of drama, a 'concentrating mirror, which, instead of weakening, concentrates and condenses the coloured rays, which makes of a mere gleam a light, and of a light a flame' (preface to *Cromwell*).

The studio/smoking room

The tapestries room gives onto the 'studio', the rear room on the right of the ground floor, work on which continued from October 1857 to 1859. Bathed by the light from its large windows looking out over the terrace and garden, the studio contrasts with the dim tapestries room. The natural light is enhanced by the monochrome Dutch stained glass with yellow borders, dated 1669 and reused in two windows, the Chinese rice-paper lantern hanging in the middle of the room, the translucent Chinese panels above the doors, the holes deliberately made in the bird tapestry to let the light through, and the gold of the circular panels painted on a black ground.

As in the tapestries room, the whole of one wall is taken up by a single, monumental composition, an assemblage of three wooden chests and table legs whose ornaments recur as leitmotifs throughout the house: the coats-of-arms of the Hugos of Lorraine and General Hugo, grotesques, rosettes, seven-branched candelabra with tripod bases, six-pointed stars, fiery wheels of Fortune, spirals, etc. These symbolic motifs seem to imbue this piece with a mysterious, syn-

11. Chantal Brière, 'Hauteville House ou le goût des inscriptions', *L'Œil de Victor Hugo*, proceedings of the colloquium, 19–21 September 2002, Musée d'Orsay, Université Paris VII (Paris, Éditions des Cendres/Musée d'Orsay, 2004) p. 231.

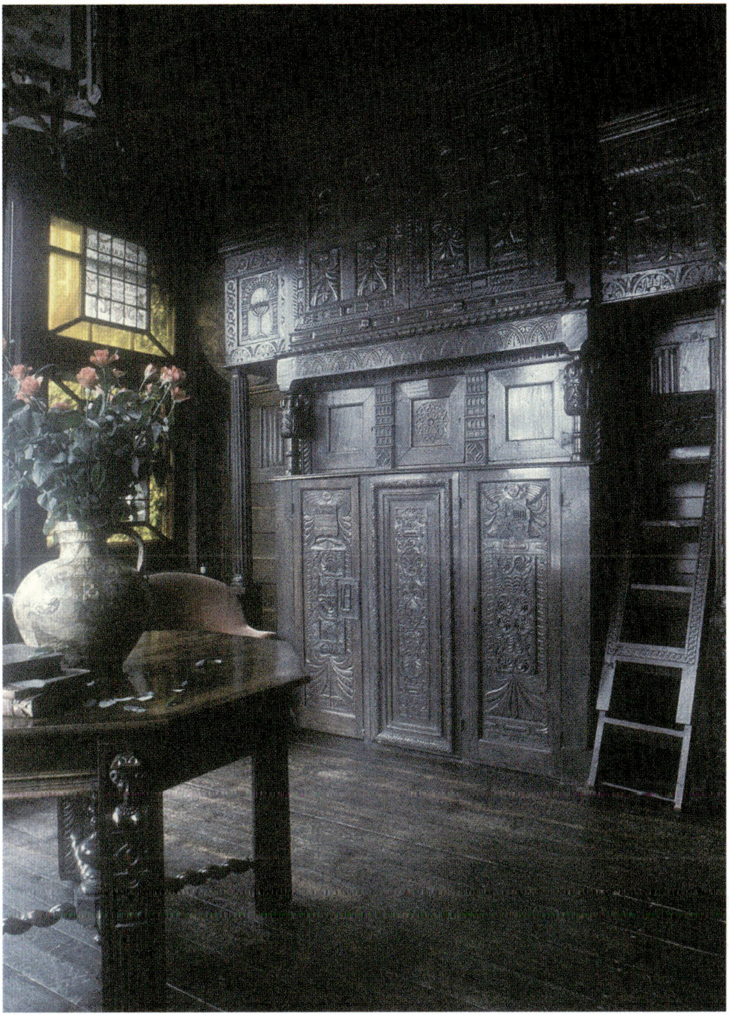

ill. 14
Joël Laiter
(born 1945)
The smoking room,
2001
Colour print on
Toscana paper
38 x 26.6 cm
MVHP-PH-4634

cretic wisdom. Above the great chest, Mauger carved the inscription *AD AUGUSTA-PER ANGUSTA'* (diary, 14 May 1859), the password of the conspirators in Hernani, a medieval phrase that can be translated as 'To high places by narrow roads'.

The corners of the octagonal table in the middle of the smoking room are decorated with grotesques, a beautiful young woman and a diabolical monster, expressions of the Hugolian alliance of the sublime and the grotesque, of darkness and light, which when associated with an hourglass, take on the role of a *vanitas*.

Victor Hugo's coat-of-arms

When he was elevated to the peerage in 1845, Victor Hugo created a coat-of-arms for himself. In 1828, after the death of his father, who had been granted the title of Count of Sigüenza by Napoleon Bonaparte's brother Joseph, he proclaimed himself a baron, and after the death of his brother Eugène in 1837, became a vicount. His coat-of-arms was composed, on the left, of the shield of the Hugos of Lorraine, from whom he thought himself to have descended, and on the right, that of his father and the battle cry, EGO HUGO ('I, Hugo'). Coats-of-arms, with their highly codified heraldic symbols, are a major decorative theme throughout Hauteville House: sculpted in the large wood composition in the studio and on the backs of the stalls in the oak gallery, depicted with studs on the leather of the coffer chair in the Garibaldi bedroom, embroidered on the armchair next to the fireplace in the blue drawing room, and elsewhere in the house. But in his use of this motif Hugo was contradicting his declaration in the final sentence of his preface to Cromwell: 'As for himself [the author], he prefers reasons to authorities; he has always cared more for arms than for coats-of-arms.'

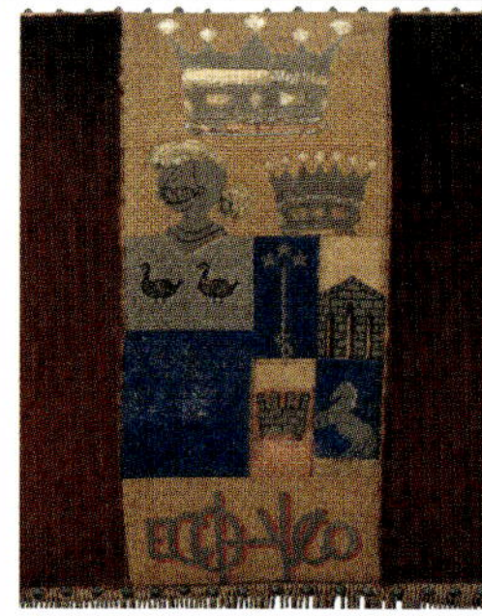

Detail of Victor Hugo's coat-of-arms, embroidered on the back of an armchair in the blue drawing room at Hauteville House (coat-of-arms drawn by Victor Hugo and embroidered by Léopoldine in 1843). Oak, silk velvet, metal, tapestry and embroidery. Inv. 2009.0.55.

A divan covered with a Caucasus carpet was placed in front of the large windows. There are similar oriental-inspired seats in the tapestries room, the billiard room and the antechamber of the lookout. In 1829, in his preface to the first edition of *Orientalia*, Victor Hugo sought sources of inspiration other than classical ones: 'Until now we have seen far too much of the modern in the century of Louis XIV, and Antiquity in Rome and Greece. Could one not see higher and further by studying the modern era in the Middle Ages and Antiquity in the Orient?' He kept this in mind in the decoration of Hauteville House, drawing extensively on these two sources of imagery and also on the 'sea[s] of poetry' of the Middle Ages and the Orient. This way of using carpets foreshadows by one and a half centuries the installations of the contemporary artist Franz West, who covers benches with carpets to encourage conviviality and relaxation.

Before they were hung in the billiard room, the pictures *ECCE* and *Justitia*, both denunciations of the death penalty, were hung for a while in this room, as indicated by a note Victor Hugo made in his diary on 7 November 1859: 'Tom has varnished the frames and placed *ECCE* and *Justitia* in the studio.'

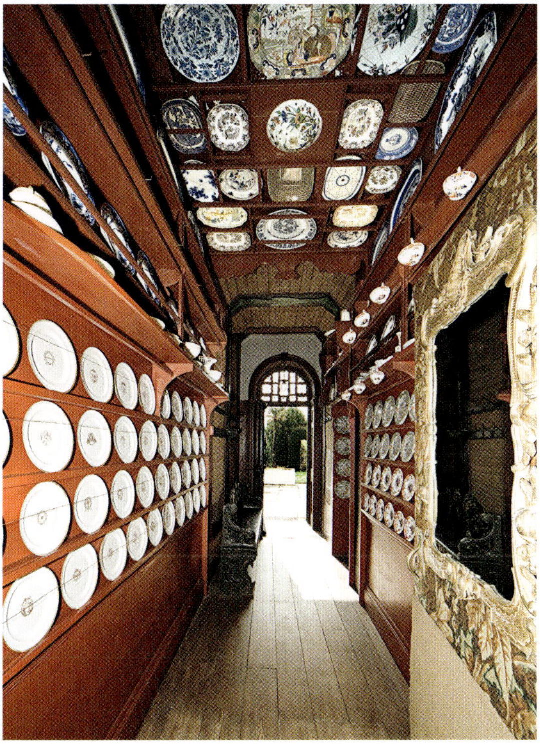

ill. 15
Hauteville House,
the faience corridor

The faience corridor

This 'kind of large dresser',[12] contrasting in its lightness with the gloomy hall, leads straight on from the *Nostre-Dame* portal to the garden. Victor Hugo encased all kinds of faience in its red-painted walls and ceiling, a principle he repeated for the decoration of Juliette Drouet's Chinese drawing room at Hauteville Fairy, now on display at the Maison de Victor Hugo in Paris.

The Sèvres porcelain service on the left-hand wall was offered to Victor Hugo by the king in 1825, as a token of gratitude for his ode, *The Coronation of Charles X*. Facing this souvenir from his artistic débuts, the mixture of ceramics on the right-hand wall, includes late 18th-century faience in the Chinese style produced by the English manufactory Mason, several purchases of which the writer mentions in his diaries. Defying the laws of gravity, this 'dresser' continues over the ceiling with dishes from China, Holland and other origins,

12. Sophie Grossiord, *Hauteville House, guide general* (Paris, Paris-Musées) 1993, p. 25.

arranged more or less symmetrically around the lid of an old-Rouen faience soup tureen, whose bowl was used as the fountain basin in the dining room.[13] This decorative utilisation of Chinese and Japanese faience stemmed from a fashion launched by Louis-Philippe at Fontainebleau.

The overall organisation of the faience corridor is not that of a space dedicated to a collection, for the display of a series of objects, but the very opposite: each object is part of an ensemble, subordinated to the whole. It was the luminosity of the ensemble, its interplay of reflections and brilliance, that interested Victor Hugo, the 'collector of all kinds of objects capable of creating ambiances'.[14]

The dining room

The first room in the house to be finished, the dining room ("*salle à manger*"), on the other side of the faience corridor, is entirely the work of Mauger, hence its nickname, the 'salle à Mauger'.[15] Victor Hugo made little mention of the room in his diaries but did numerous preparatory drawings for it. In 1857 he noted the date of the hanging of the trammel, a year after work on the house had begun: '14 [May] – inauguration of the dining room. With us six of the family, dined the French exiles Terrier, Ribeyrolles, Guérin, Duverdier, Preveraud, Kesler, Cahaigne and Lefèvre, and Mesdames Duverdier, Preveraud, mesdemoiselles Allix, Nicolle, Loysel, monsieur Marquand, editor of the *Gazette de Guernsey*, and Mr Talbot, English, director of the *Star*.'

The dining room is a bright room, whose decoration alternates light and dark. On the walls: dark wood and white faience with blue and violet motifs, dark oak panelling and windows opening onto the sky and garden; on the ceiling: polished panelling and a dominantly light-hued Gobelins tapestry.

Our attention is immediately drawn to the double 'H' in faience tiles majestically crowning the fireplace, for which the writer made many preparatory drawings. 'H' for Hauteville House, for Hugo and even Hugo's House, but also 'H' for those major Hugolian themes and

13. There is the same decorative use of crockery on the ceiling of Bartholdi's house at Colmar, a repeat of the decoration in the dining room of his apartment in rue d'Assas in Paris, where he lived from 1892.
14. Corinne Charles, *Victor Hugo. Visions d'intérieurs, du meuble au décor* (Paris, Paris-Musées, 2003) p. 46.
15. Charles Hugo, *Chez Victor Hugo par un passant*, *op. cit.*

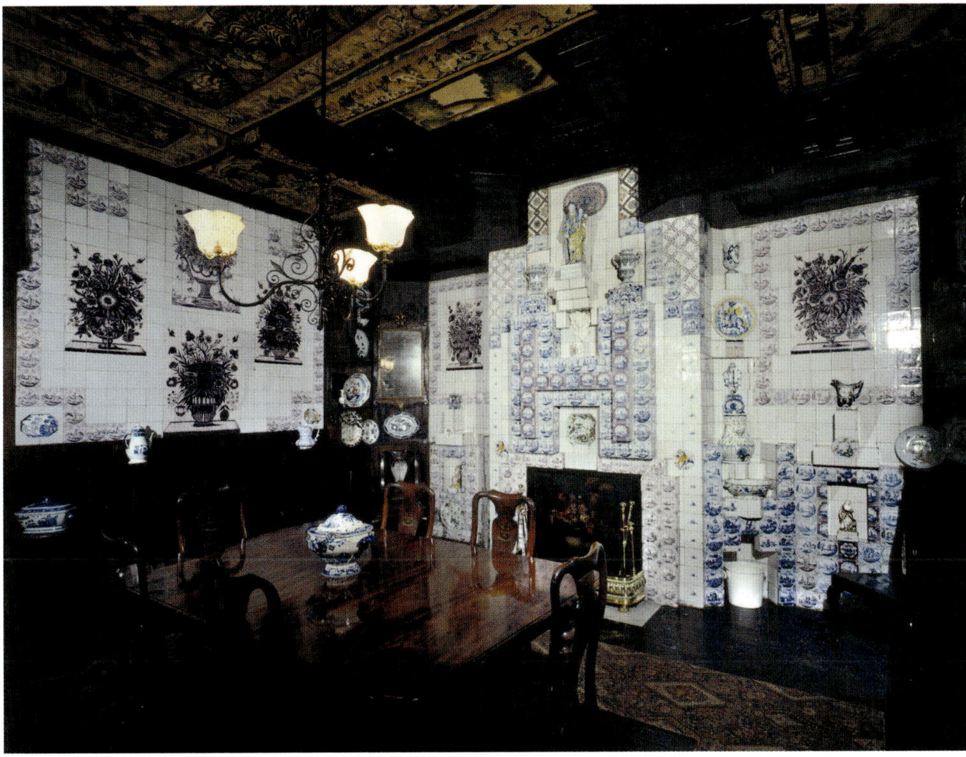

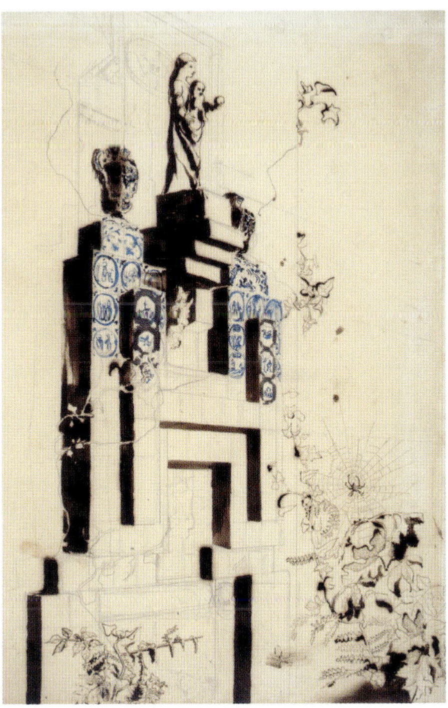

ill. 16
Victor Hugo
(1802–85)
Fireplace in the dining room at Hauteville House
Pen, brown ink wash, graphite and blue ink on watermarked verge paper
48.5 x 31.3 cm
MVHP-D-85

ill. 17
Hauteville House, the dining room

preoccupations, Homme, Héros and Humanité.'[16] The double H placed in the room where the family gathered most frequently for meals, 'unequivocally imposed the hand of the master of the house and its decoration.'[17] It marked the beginning of the identification of the man with the place whose initial they shared, and symbolises the dissemination of Hugo's identity throughout his home. It creates 'the singular, symmetrical, direct, almost consubstantial union of a man and an edifice' described by the novelist in *Notre-Dame de Paris* (IV, 5).

The double 'H' is surmounted by an old-Rouen faience statuette (dated 1756) offered to Victor Hugo by Juliette Drouet, the statuette of Our Lady of Charity, the popular Madonna and Child, whose halo here is a converted soup dish. The writer transformed her into Liberty, as indicated by the verse inscribed on the architrave:
'The people is small but will be big.
In your sacred arms, O fertile mother,
O holy Liberty with conquering stride,
You are carrying the child that carries the world.'

It was under her aegis, from March 1862, shortly before the publication of the first part of *Les Misérables*, that Hugo hosted his twice-monthly 'poor children's dinner', a full meal with a meat course for twelve poor children. In under a year, the number of guests rose to forty. Until 1870, the writer also prepared a Christmas tree for the island's poverty-stricken children, around which he offered them sweets and clothes. 'I am not averse to people saying that in exile Victor Hugo's door is ajar to the rich and wide open to the poor', he wrote in the postscript to a letter to his wife on 22 March 1862.
Time seems to have stood still in the dining room, a timelessness materialised by the two empty clock cases reused in the decoration and especially by the *Cella patrum defunctorum*, sanctuary of dead ancestors, called the 'seat of the ancestors' not far from the guests. This imposing high-backed medieval throne surmounted by a dais, finished by Mauger on 19 January 1857, recalls the invisible presence of the deceased and concretises the inscription *ABSENTES ADSUNT* ('The absent are present') on the lower back. The writer

16. Florian Rodari, 'Un espace chiffré', in Danielle Molinari and Françoise Heilbrun (ed.) *En collaboration avec le soleil. Victor Hugo, photographies de l'exil*, exh. cat. (Paris, Maison de Victor Hugo/Musée d'Orsay, 1998) p. 176.
17. Chantal Brière, *Victor Hugo et le roman architectural*, *op. cit.*, p. 502.

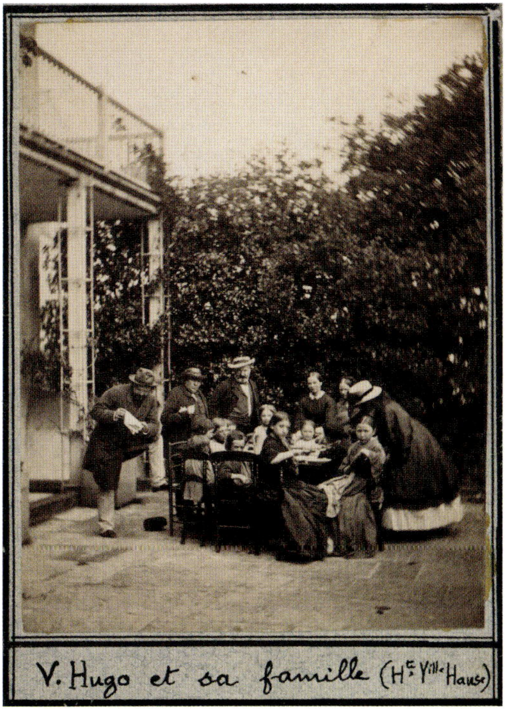

ill. 18
Edmond Bacot
(1814–75)
Victor Hugo and his family at one of the dinners for poor children at Hauteville House, 1862
Albumen print
8.9 x 6.6 cm
MVHP-PH-2555

designed this chair while he was working on *Eviradnus* (*The Legend of the Ages*), chapter VII of which, 'The Dining Room', seems to echo the *Cella patrum defunctorum*:
'What would be strange in this dark and dreamy place
Would be that the one we are waiting for was alive.'

But it is perhaps *The Universal Prayer*, a poem in *Autumn Leaves* (XXXVII, 15 June 1830), that casts more light on the armchair's meaning – as a materialisation of the memory's struggle against oblivion, as a means of bringing the dead back to life:
'Pray! That the father, the uncle and the ancestors,
Who demand more than merely our prayers,
Shudder in their graves when they hear themselves named,
Knowing that on earth we still remember.'

Like a pulpit, the armchair's sacred dimension is accentuated by the religious iconography and philosophical inscriptions decorating it. The gilt plaque on the upper part of the back depicts Christ and the Good Samaritan, surmounted by a wooden statuette of the Virgin Mary. On 19 February 1859 Victor Hugo engraved the Latin pronouns

HIC/ NIHIL/ ALIAS/ ALIQUID ('Nothing here, something elsewhere'), evoking the presence of the deceased in another world, while the sentence *PULVIS/ ES CINIS/ SUM* ('You are dust, I am ashes'), inscribed on either side of the Virgin Mary, emphasises the fleetingness of earthly existence. The other inscriptions are dedicated to Victor Hugo's ancestors: *GEORGES/ 1534*, the earliest, on the right armrest, and *JOSEPH LEOPOLD SIGISBET/ 1828* (date of his death) on the left. The coat-of-arms of the Hugos of Lorraine dominates the upper half of the back, above the Virgin Mary, accompanied by the motto *EGO HUGO* and echoed in the ostentatious 'H' formed by the legs and cross-strut.

The entire chair repeats the 'H' of the fireplace and, according to this passage from *Heap of Stones*: 'Words have a figure. The armchair is a capital "H" seen from the front, and a small "h" seen from one side.'

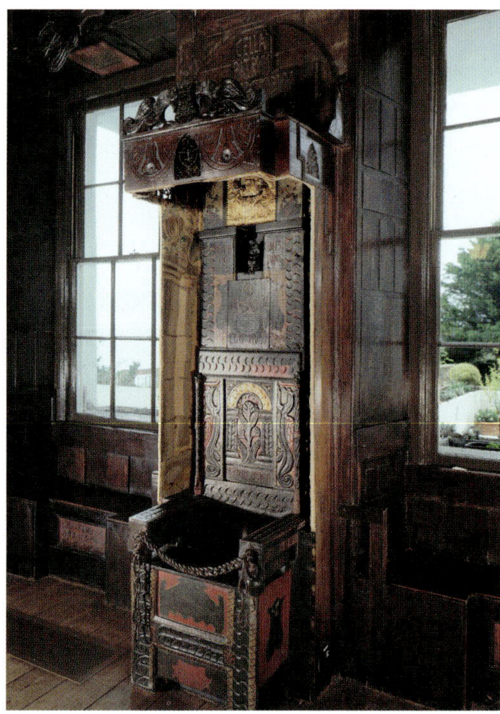

ill. 19
Hauteville House,
the dining room,
the ancestors' chair

The Architecture-Writing / The Writing-Architecture

'Architecture began like all writing, first as an alphabet'[18] before becoming words, phrases, formulae. One could thus say that Hauteville House condenses, in the true sense of the word, all the stages of architecture-writing: from the 'H' to the Latin phrases present throughout the house, especially in the dining room.

Text is often placed at strategic and focal points, on doors and fireplaces, as part of a veritable 'typographic *mise en scène*'.[19]

Exile is present on the walls as one enters the dining room, the room containing the most texts: *EXILIUM VITA EST* ('Life is an exile' or 'Exile is life').

Like a huge book, the house progressively unveils the moral precepts guiding the lives of its inhabitants. On two benches in the dining room: *LEVER A VI, DINER A X/ SOUPER A VI, COUCHER A X/ FAICT VIVRE LHOMME X FOIS X* [...] and *POST CAENAM ST/ ABIS SEU PASSUS M/ ILLE MEABIS VALE* ('After a meal, stand or take a thousand paces. Carry yourself well').

The Latin sentence on the ceiling recalls the vanity of all earthly dwellings, and of Hauteville House: *TU QUI TRANSIS PER DOMOS PERITURAS SIS MEMOR DOMUS AETERNAE* ('In your transit through perishable residences, do not forget the eternal home').

The values espoused by the master of the house are incorporated into the room itself: *HOMO* (man), *POPULUS* (people), by the windows.

Furniture and objects also have their word to say. The chairs around the large table bear the crest of the Tuppers, a prominent Guernsey family, and their motto, 'Hope is my strength', doubly meaningful in the context of exile. The seeds of possible narratives are sown by words on objects purchased from antique dealers: *widow* on a statuette of a weeping woman, and *hanibal 1624* on a dish.

Two words are present throughout the house: Victor Hugo's name, 'that militant name, that care-worn name, the exile's name',[20] whose repeated affirmation is a means of combating absence and death, and the initials 'V.H.', which 'lend themselves to many constructions because [they] concentrate the essential lines of space, the vertical, the horizontal and the diagonal'.[21]

18. Victor Hugo, *Notre-Dame de Paris*, 'Ceci tuera cela'.
19. Chantal Brière, *Victor Hugo et le roman architectural*, *op. cit.*, p. 550.
20. Letter from Victor Hugo to Jules Janin, 16 August 1856.
21. Chantal Brière, *Victor Hugo et le roman architectural*, *op. cit.*, p. 512.

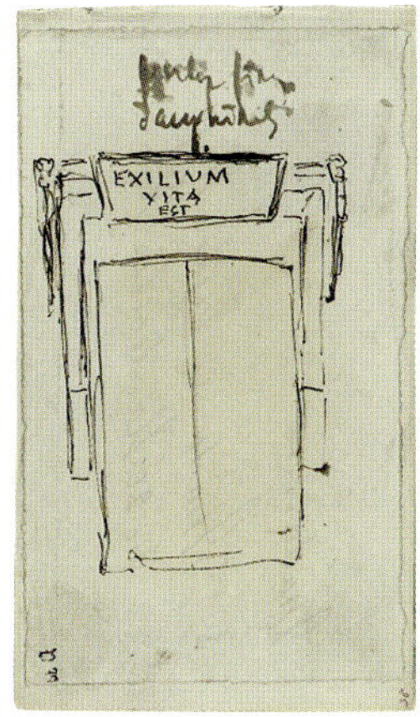

Victor Hugo
(1802–85)
"Exilium Vita Est"
Brown ink on paper
7.6 x 13.2 cm
Handwritten inscriptions above: 'perles fines/ dauphines'?
Glued by Victor Hugo in a book of 'Rough drawings', mostly related to the decoration of Hauteville House
MVHP-D-1393 f° 25

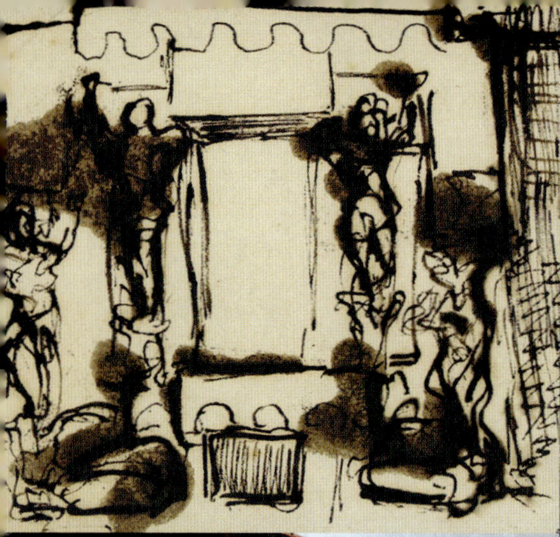
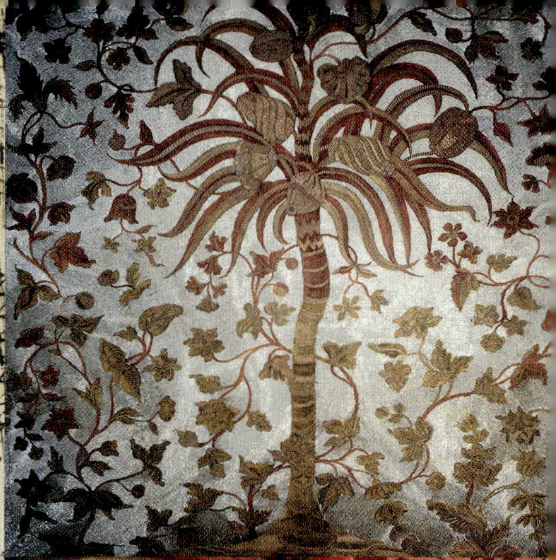
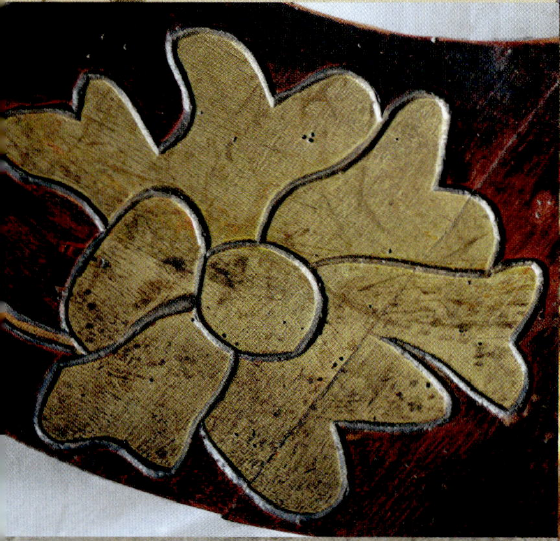
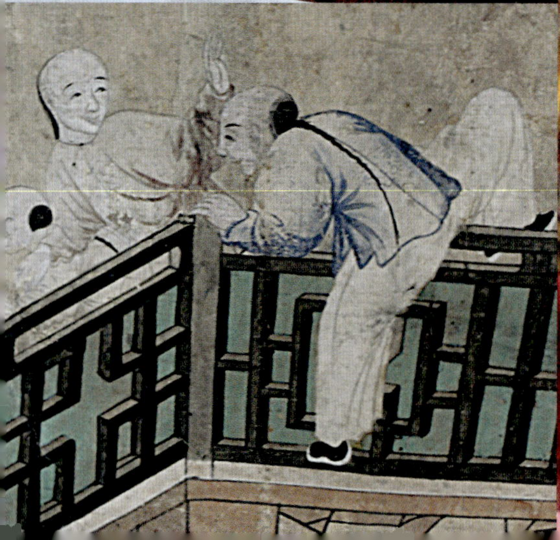
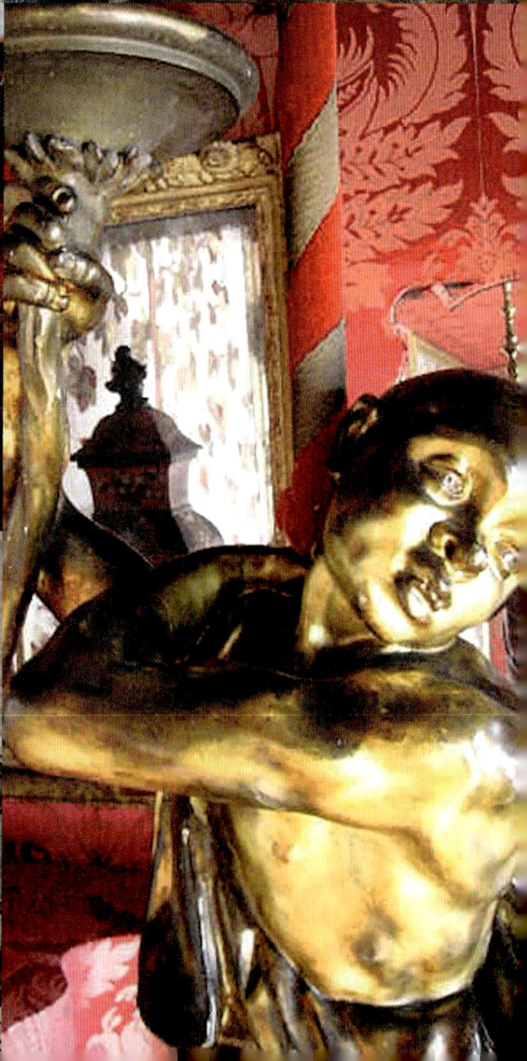

First floor

The staircase leads up to the landing, from which, on the right, one enters the former bedrooms of Madame Hugo and Adèle, and on the left, two large drawing rooms looking out over the garden. The lightness of the landing, hung with 'blue and yellow-striped brocatelle',[22] is heightened by two mirrors and the oculus lit by a lamp which Hugo called 'Fanfan' as a tribute to Paul Meurice's drama *Fanfan la Tulipe* (1858). The regular ticking of a clock accompanies visitors during their gradual ascension towards the light.

On the left, the red and blue drawing rooms, work on which continued until 1857 and February 1859 respectively. According to Mme Hugo, their decoration was inspired by the Masserano Palace in Madrid, which had fascinated Victor Hugo during his childhood, and which she described as follows: 'Drawing room hung with red damask, boudoir hung with light blue damask [...]. Nothing but gilding, sculptures, Bohemian glass and Chinese and Japanese vases.'[23] This magnificence explains both Hauteville House's reputation on Guernsey 'as a palace of The Thousand and One Nights',[24] and François-Victor's dissatisfaction when he wrote to his mother in May 1859: '[...] after the mistake to give over the half of this large house to drawing rooms and reception rooms. The prime role of a house is not to be beautiful but hospitable. Any inhospitable house misses its duty, isn't it your opinion?'[25] Nonetheless, beauty and hospitality seem to have been reconciled in these two drawing rooms.

22. Victor Hugo, 2ND DIARY, f° 21, 8 March 1858.
23. Adèle Hugo, *Victor Hugo raconté par un témoin de sa vie*, vol. I, chap. XIX, Maison de Victor Hugo, Paris, MVHP-ms-α4783.
24. Jean Delalande, *Victor Hugo à Hauteville House* (Paris, Albin Michel) 1947.
25. Maison de Victor Hugo, Paris, MVHP-ms-α315.

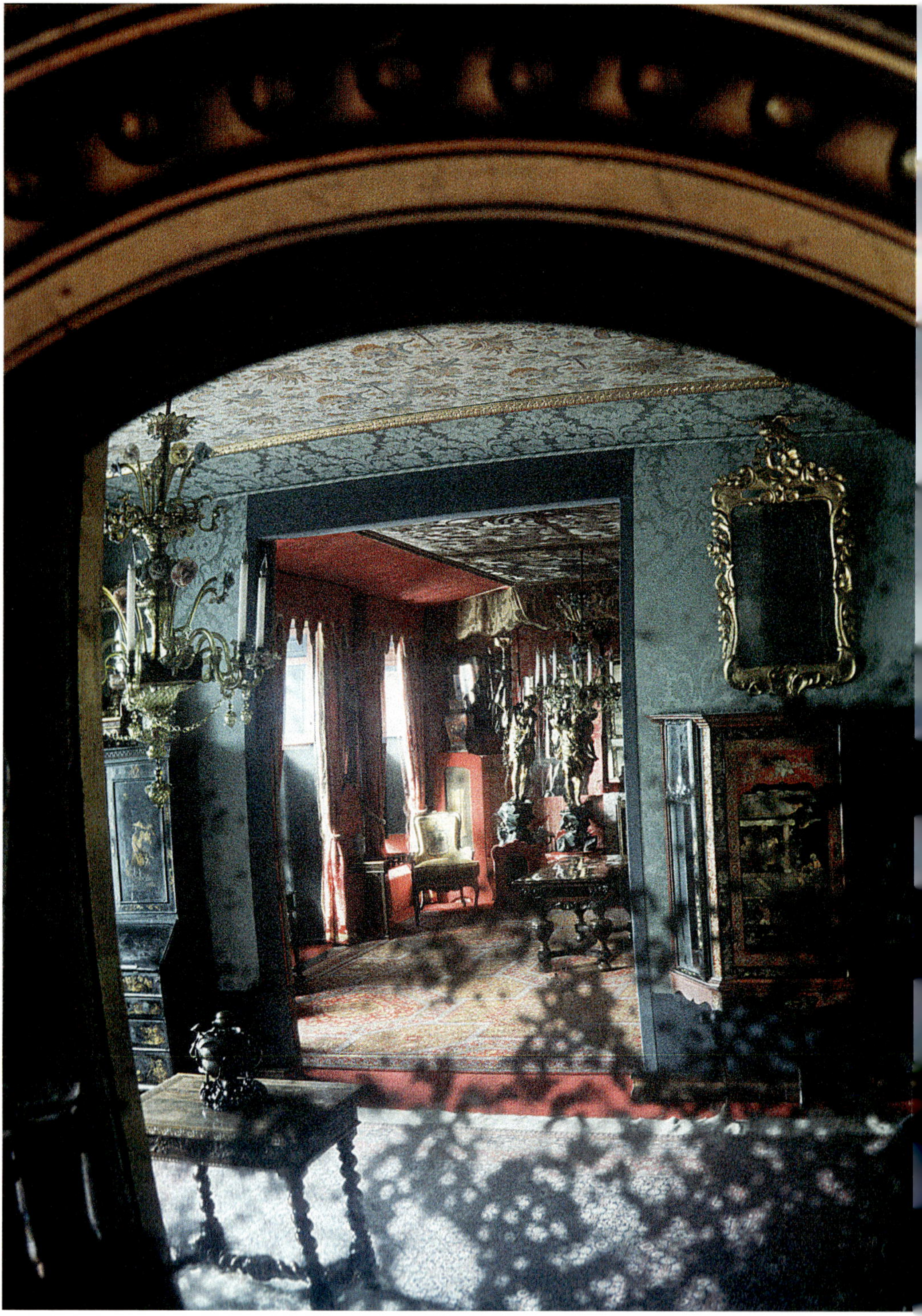

The red drawing room

'After dinner we usually retired to the sumptuous décor of the large drawing room hung with damask, where there are tapestries in white jet, silk and gold, and the gold of the torchères on the fireplace. The warm scent, which wafts in from the nearby conservatory, full of heavy bunches of red grapes, hangs in the room and mingles with the smell of the old furniture. During these evenings, which for us were moments of unforgettable charm, my grandfather used to tell us tales. Sitting in his armchair, he would take us between his knees and speak to us closely.'

Georges Hugo, *My Grandfather*, Paris, Calmann-Lévy, 1902, p. 41.

ill. 20
Joël Laiter
(born 1945)
The blue drawing room in the concave mirror, 2001
Colour print on Dyson paper
39.8 x 26.5 cm
MVHP-PH-3895

The red drawing room is the most opulent room in the house, at once luminous, shimmering, lively, ostentatious, enchanting, baroque, welcoming, illusionist and theatrical.

Here again, it is the fireplace at the end of the room that first catches the eye, flanked by four giltwood *porte-torchères* that seem almost to be greeting us. They were brought from the apartment at 37 rue de La-Tour-d'Auvergne, where the Hugos lived just before their exile. Sculpted in the 16th century, they are thought to have once decorated the Bucentaur, the state galley that was taken out into the Adriatic each year, and from whose upper gallery the Doges performed the ceremony of wedding Venice to the sea.

The walls are decorated with four large embroideries of gilt and copper thread and chenille on a ground of glass beads, 'a damascening of fire on a canvas of light'.[26] They were bought from an antique dealer in rue de Lappe in Paris and, legend has it, came from Christina of Sweden's rooms in the Château de Fontainebleau, where they would have witnessed the murder of her lover, Monaldeschi. Two embroideries hang symmetrically on either side of the door: *The Cock and the Pearl*, an illustration of La Fontaine's fable, and another depicting an eagle at the foot of a tree on which an eaglet is perching. The motifs of the two embroideries on the ceiling, plant

26. Charles Hugo, preliminary notes for Hetzel, 1859 (Bibliothèque nationale) for *Chez Victor Hugo par un passant*, *op. cit.*, quoted by Martine Écalle, in *Perles et broderies chez Victor Hugo* (Ville de Paris, Maison de Victor Hugo, Hauteville House, 1972-1973) unnumbered.

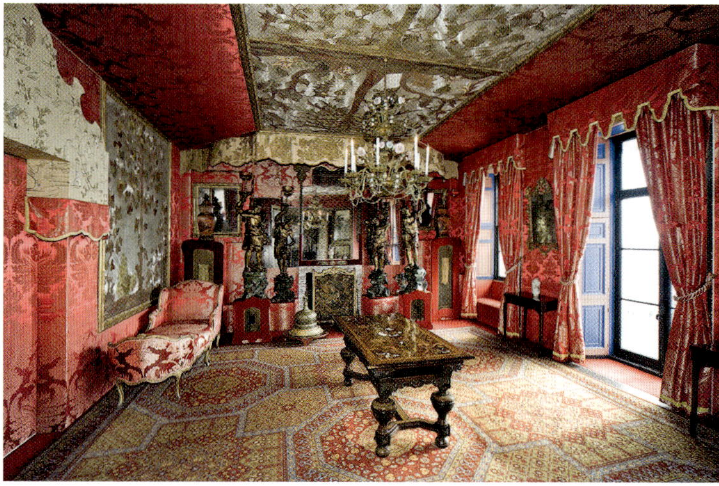

ill. 21
Hauteville house,
the red drawing room

ill. 22
Arsène Garnier
(1822–1900)
Victor Hugo standing in front of the fireplace in the red drawing room, Hauteville House, 1868
Albumen print
17 x 12.8 cm
Dedicated to Victor Hugo by Arsène Garnier: 'D'un humble artiste/ Au plus grand des poètes/ A Victor Hugo./ A. Garnier, Guernesey. Avril 1868' [From a humble artist to the greatest of poets, to Victor Hugo, A. Garnier, Guernsey, April 1868']
MVHP-PH-1319

compositions around a tropical tree, are reminiscent of the chintz wall hangings painted in India for the European market during the Mughal Empire in the early 18th century.

Chinese lacquer panels, their tints echoing the room's red and gold harmonies, open onto the blue drawing room, revealing their blue-hued reverse side. These panels were among the first Chinese works Victor Hugo acquired, and already decorated his Parisian apartment before his exile. In summer, the double doors were sometimes opened wide to transform both drawing rooms into a single gallery more than twelve metres long, further enlarged by the play of reflections in the mirrors at either end.

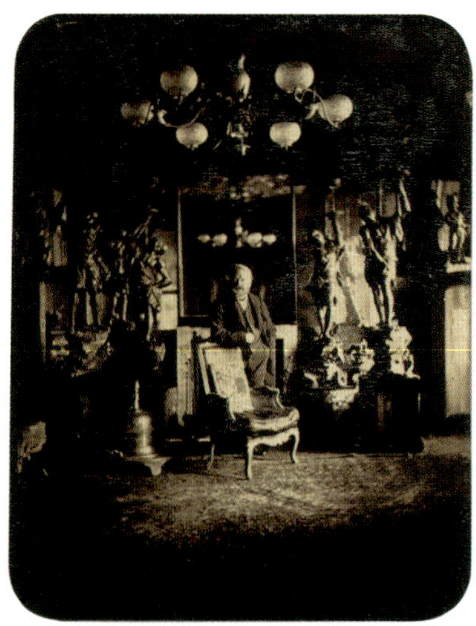

The blue drawing room

The blue drawing room echoes as a subdued, dreamlike echo of the dazzling fantasy of the red drawing room.

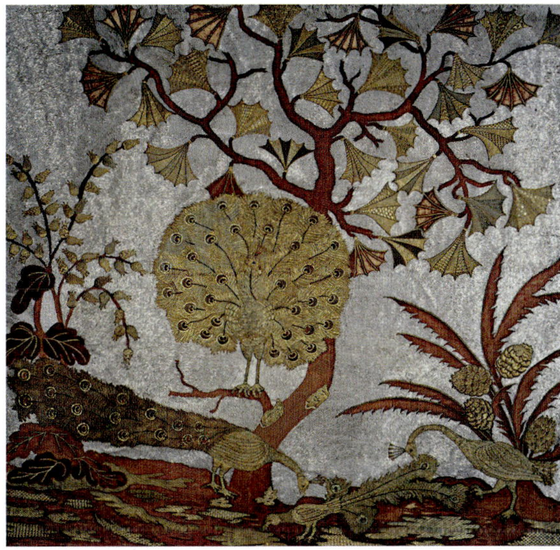

ill. 23
Anonymous
The Jay Dressed in Peacock's Feathers
Canvas covered with metal, gold, copper, silk and linen chenille, glass bead embroidery
2.40 x 2.49 m
Tapestry, hanging in the blue drawing room, Hauteville House

Here again, the master of the house attached a legend to most of the objects in the room to give them an illustrious aura. The gilt wreathed columns symmetrically framing the fireplace with the *porte-torchères*, are said to have come from the bed of Madame de Maintenon. Gustave Larroumet, who visited Hauteville House in the late 19th century, wrote that Victor Hugo 'baptised and debaptised, not always remembering the original provenance of all these objects and didn't hesitate to give them a grandiose, bizarre, terrifying or amusing history'.[27] The sumptuous Chinese silks which originally decorated both drawing rooms were replaced in 1956. Although in his letter to Captain Butler on 25 November 1861, Victor Hugo condemned the sacking of the Summer Palace, he wasn't averse to profiting from its pillage, if one is to believe the note he made in his diary on 23 March 1865: 'Bought the entire lot of Chinese silks from an English officer who took part in the expedition and who had taken it from the Summer Palace of the Emperor of China – 360 [F].'

It is the objects' iconography, rather than their origin, which tells stories. The pearl embroidery in the blue drawing room illustrates La Fontaine's fable *The Jay Dressed in Peacock's Feathers*. The choice of this fable, similar to the *Cock and the Pearl*, could well have been to deflate the ostentatiousness of the two drawing rooms and recall the playfulness, fantasy and liberty in their decoration. As elsewhere in the house, Victor Hugo, the inspired handyman and *metteur en scène*,

27. Gustave Larroumet, *La Maison de Victor Hugo. Impressions guernesiaises* (Paris, Honoré Champion, 1895) p. 30.

had no qualms about reusing the most heterogeneous objects for other purposes to create an overall effect. The upper part of the mantels of both fireplaces are inset with an unexpected feature, chosen for its brilliance: in the red drawing room, a band of metal decorated with garnet-coloured and green grotesques, offered by the Hungarian count Teleki, in exile like Hugo; and a small silver dish in the blue drawing room.

Two objects linked to the charity sale Madame Hugo organised in the spring of 1860 graced the drawing room: the lotus-shaped bronze incense burner Alexandre Dumas donated, and the table with inkwells created with a view to funding a crèche, comprising three inkwells, a lighter and four signed letters donated by Hugo, Dumas, Lamartine and George Sand (now in the Maison de Victor Hugo in Paris). Victor Hugo finally bought both these objects himself. Charity sales were widespread in the 19th century, particularly in the Channel Islands, and for Hugo were a means of responding in concrete terms to the preface of *Les Misérables*, and also of consolidating his place in Guernsey society.

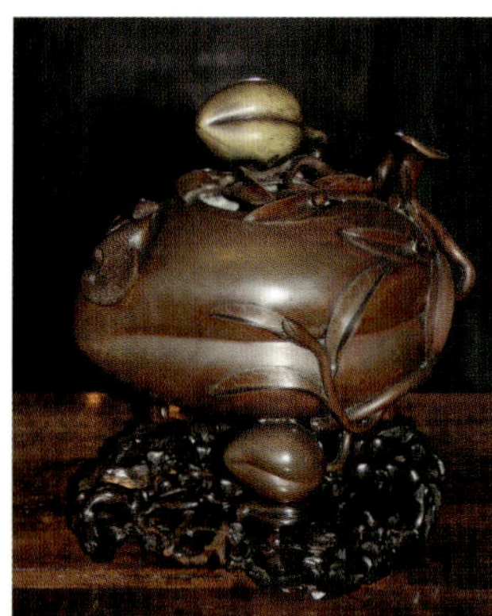

ill. 24
Incense burner offered by Alexandre Dumas to Victor Hugo, blue drawing room, Hauteville House
Bronze
Plinth:
5.5 x 25.5 x 22 cm;
pot: 22 x 24 cm;
lid: 7 x 12 x 11.5 cm

The Far East

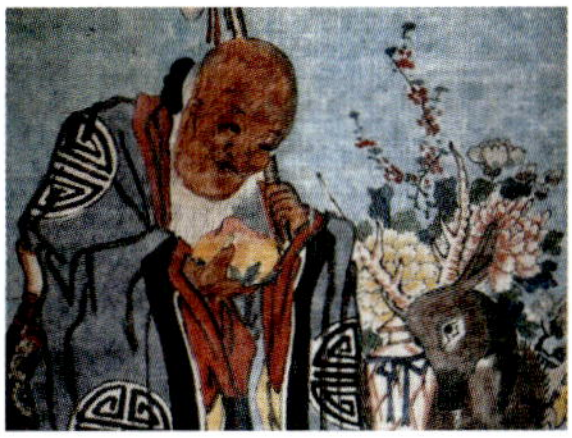

Anonymous
Shou-Lao
Painting on rice paper
74 X 129.5 cm
Detail of a panel on the door of the blue drawing room, Hauteville House

'A blue porcelain vase with a strange form
Gleaming with peacocks fanning wide their tails,
The beautiful azure land of which the Chinese dream.'

Victor Hugo, *Sunlight and Shadows*, IV, 24-29 June 1839

Victor Hugo's taste for all things oriental had been fuelled by the European craze for *chinoiseries* since the 18th century. In his diaries, he mentions numerous purchases of objects from China (figurines, mirrors, chest, blinds, vases, clocks, lanterns, frames, etc.), India (paintings, matting) and Japan (crockery, lamps). He bought them from English and Guernsian antique dealers, from Lyons, Jeune and Henry via the intermediary of his sons, and from Forward, Madame Harmel and Masters. He also bought objects directly from their owners, received gifts and exchanged pieces.
An avid collector of objects decorated with monsters, chimera and fables that could fuel his imagination, he was also interested in far-eastern spirituality. In his library at Hauteville House he had the *Sacred Books of the Orient* (1841, Pauthier de Censay), which includes *The Shu Jing* or 'Classic of History', the 'Four Books' of Confucius and his disciples and other translations of major religious texts with accompanying notes by the great orientalists of the time.
The red and blue drawing rooms are the most Chinese rooms in the house: Fu dog vases and chest, wallpapers, silks, idol in an armchair, folding hexagonal table, panels, etc., give them their far-eastern look. We are witnessing the encounter between the pomp and exuberance of Chinese art and the aesthetic sensibility of Victor Hugo the interior designer, who created a Chinese drawing room for Juliette Drouet at Hauteville Fairy in 1864. The symbolism of the figures caters to his love of stories. The Chinese panel on the door of the blue drawing room, for example, portrays the god of longevity Shu Lao. Holding a peach, Taoist symbol of immortality, and carrying a double gourd on his stick, he symbolises the communication between the earthly and immortal worlds, and is accompanied by a deer and a bat, emblems of happiness. The alliance of the sublime and the grotesque and the romantic will to resolve dualities have an equivalent in Chinese Taoist wisdom, which advocates the reconciliation of opposites, in an 'inextricable mixture of celestial and infernal elements'.[28]
Japanese art, far less exuberant, and whose use in decoration in Europe became fashionable later on, from the 1860s onwards, influenced Hugo primarily in his painted decorations on wood, in which he makes masterful use of the void and stylisation of nature.

28. Jean Biès, 'Hauteville House ou le caravansérail de la rêverie', *Europe*, no. 671, March 1985, p. 147.

The conservatory

ill. 25
Hauteville House, the conservatory

ill. 26
Edmond Bacot
(1814–75)
Victor Hugo and Hennett de Kesler in the conservatory, Hauteville House,
1862
Albumen print
8.4 x 6 cm
MVHP-PH-1322 (1)

The glass architecture of the conservatory brings nature into the house, opening it up to the sky outside. A grape vine formerly grew on the trelliswork decorated with the 'VH' monogram, providing welcome shade in summer and grapes for the family and guests. In this room bathed in light and greenery all the year round, Victor Hugo recreated the atmosphere of the greenhouse at Marine Terrace.

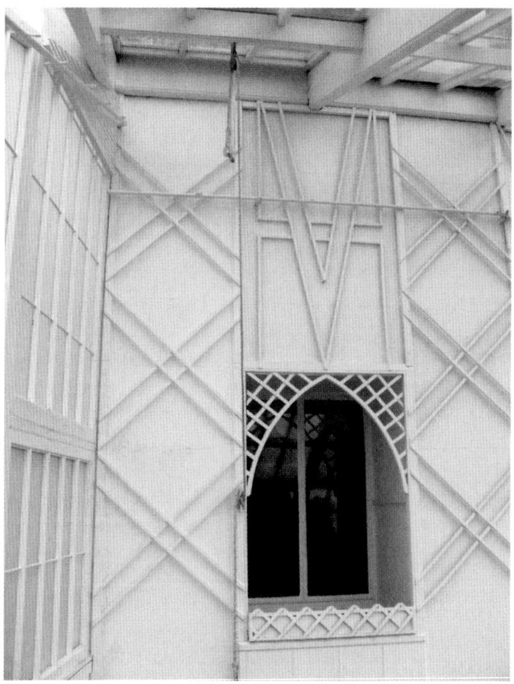

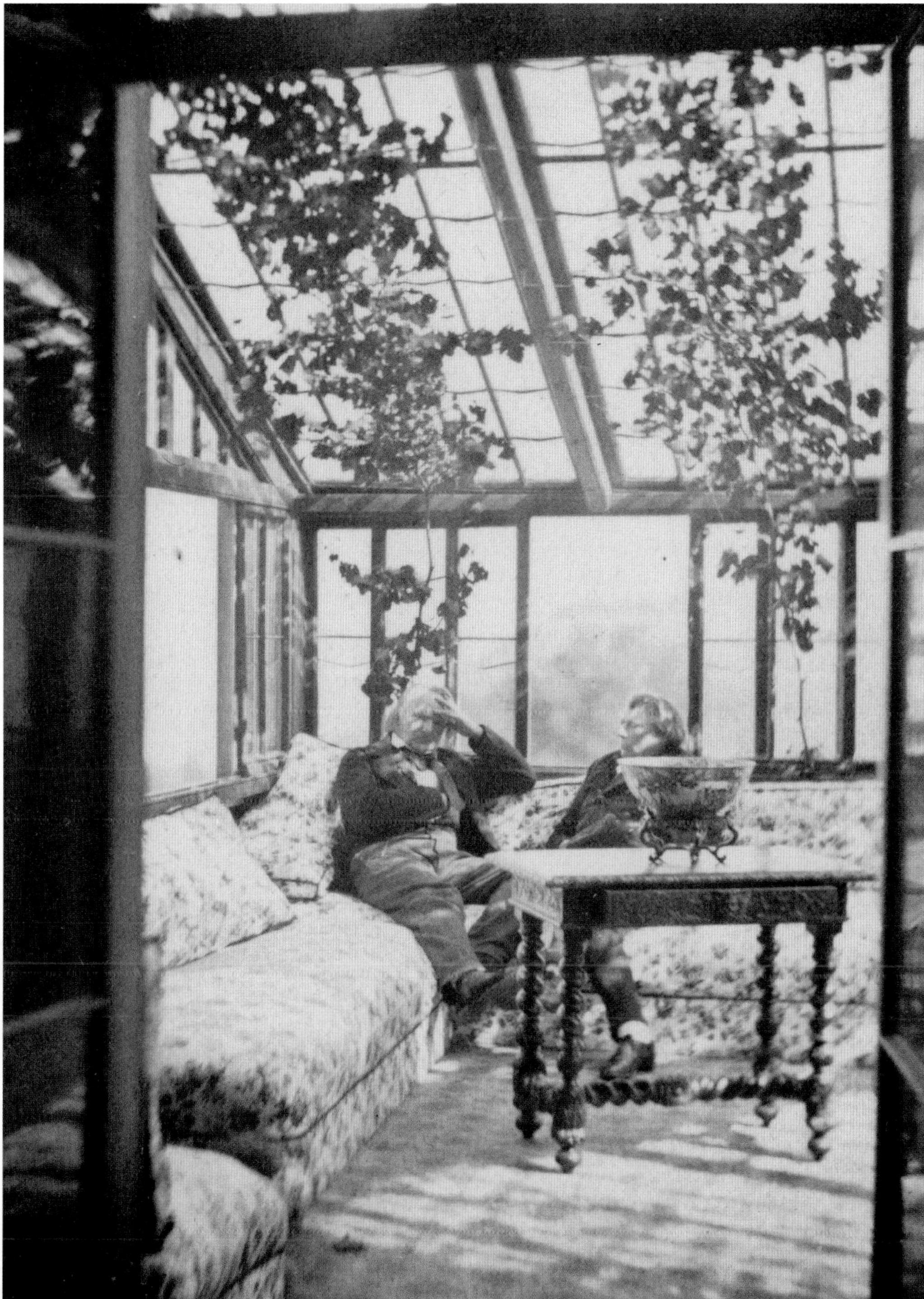

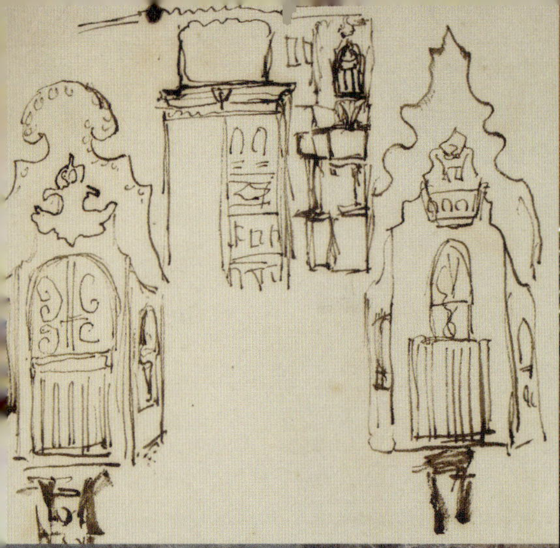

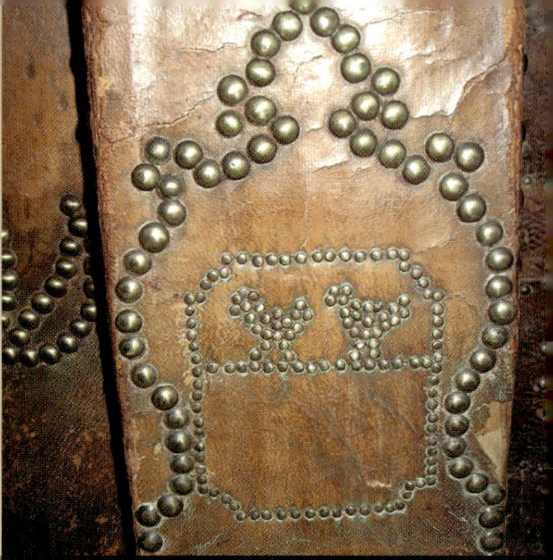

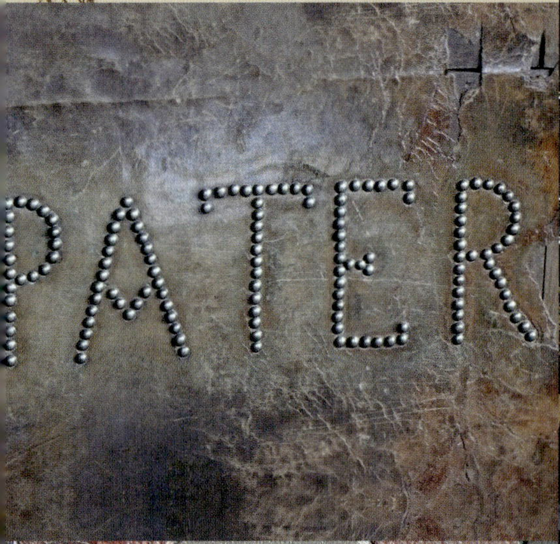
PATER

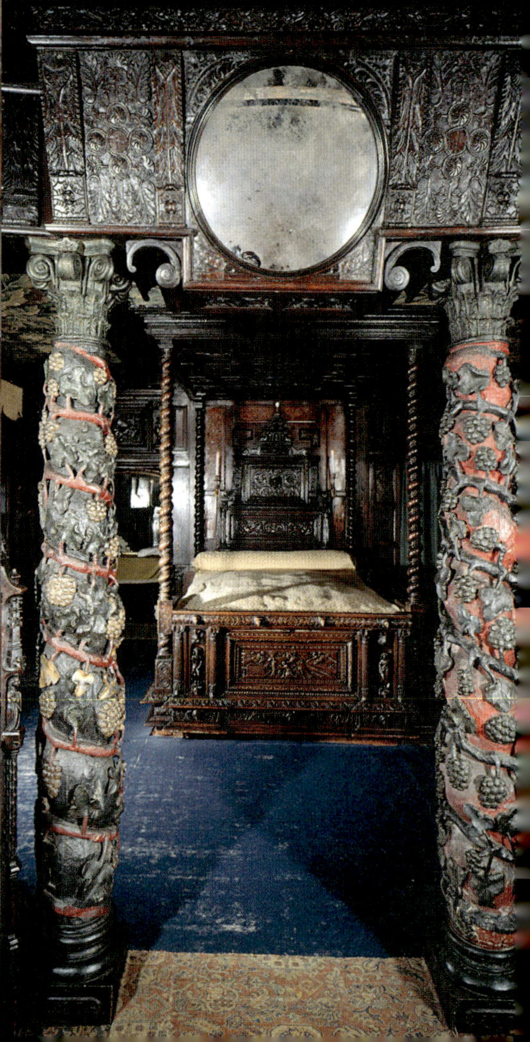

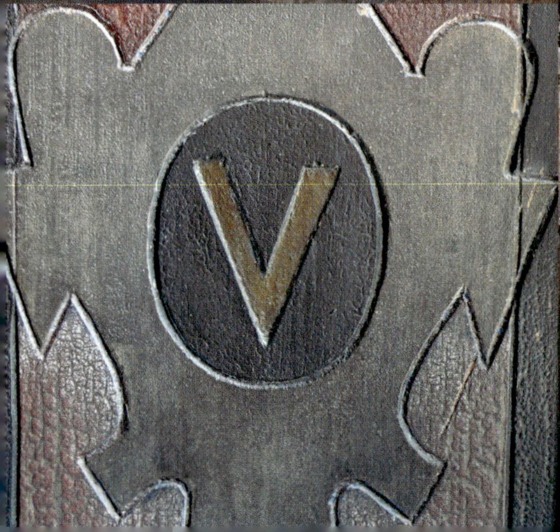
V

Second floor

A well of light, reflected by a large mirror, guides the visitor up towards the second floor of Hauteville House. The skylight at the top is set in a wooden drum surrounded by a gilt frame, on which Victor Hugo painted plant motifs, butterflies and birds recalling the decoration of the frames of his drawings in the billiard room. A garland of flowers, leaves and birds, surmounted by a female angel in a small trompe-l'œil frame ensures the transition between the house and nature outside. Hugo discreetly signed his work *DEUS DIES* ('God, day') in gold letters outlined in black, thereby stating the cosmic communion between artist and nature and the continuity between his residence and the universe. The decoration of the rotunda was begun on 29 May 1862 and finished on 9 July. The large Gobelins tapestries, *Spring* and *Summer*, on the circular landing, echo the decoration of the skylight above.

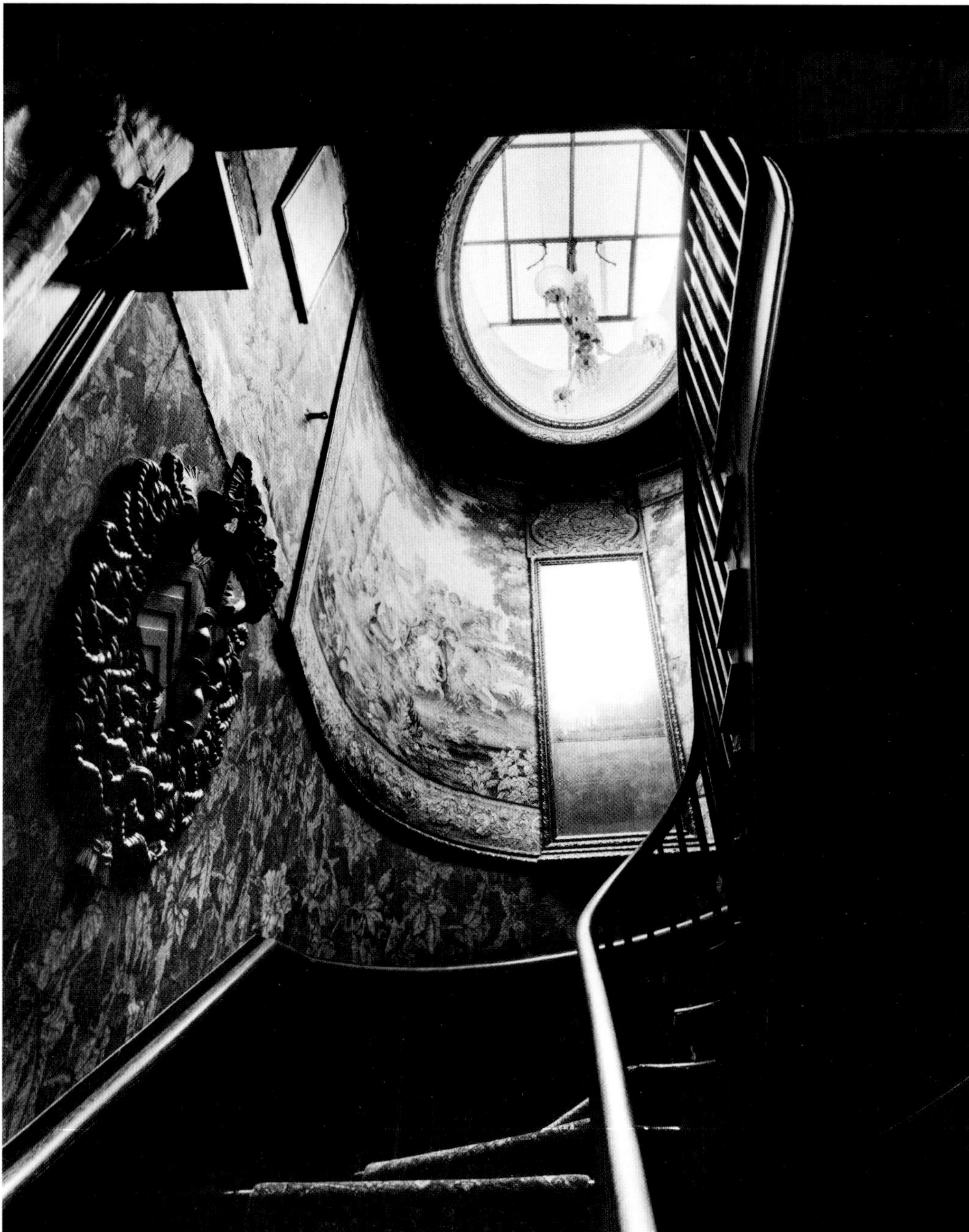

ill. 27
Olivier Mériel (born 1955)
Hauteville, the staircase, Tuesday 17 March 1998, 1 p.m. to 2:15 p.m.
Contact print
375 x 28.5 cm
MVHP-PH-2644

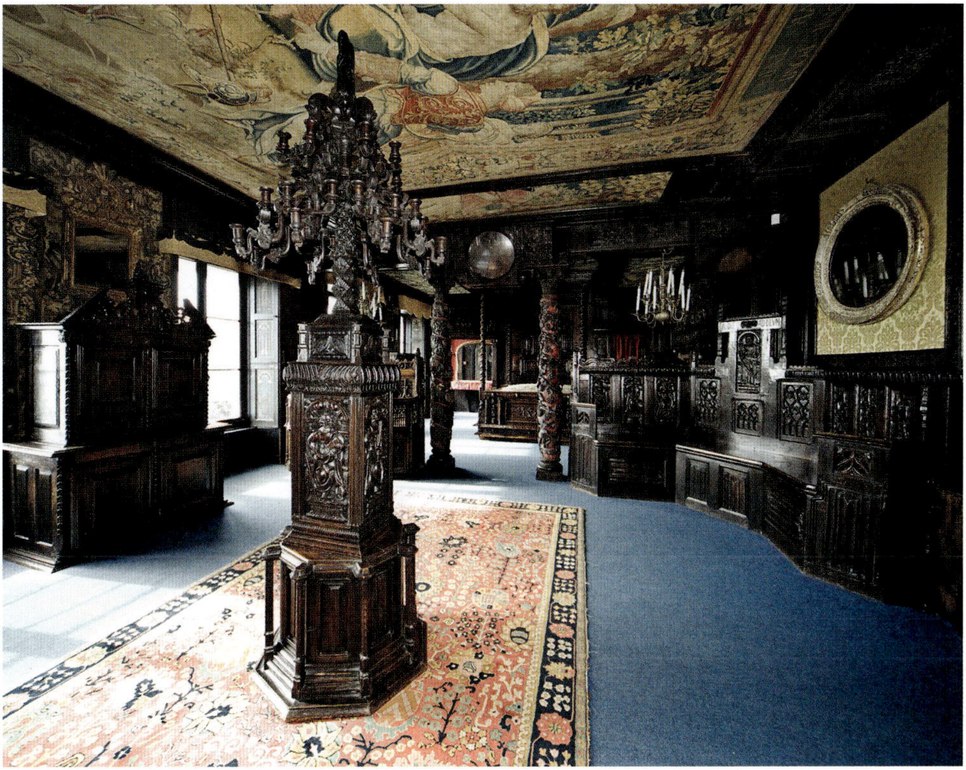

The oak gallery

The entire garden side of the second floor is taken up by the oak gallery, a 'veritable forest of sculpted oak'.[29] Work on it continued until September 1859, with a pause from January to March 1858. Its two, hieratic, severe rooms were the master of the house's study and bedroom. Yet he slept in this bedroom only for a short time, during a serious throat illness in 1861, usually working on the floor above. Two wooden cabled columns, *Tristitia* (*Sadness*) and *Laetitia* (*Joy*), installed in September 1857, frame the doorway between these two spaces.

ill 28
Hauteville House, the oak gallery

29. René Weiss, *La Maison de Victor Hugo à Guernesey*, *op. cit.*, p. 54.

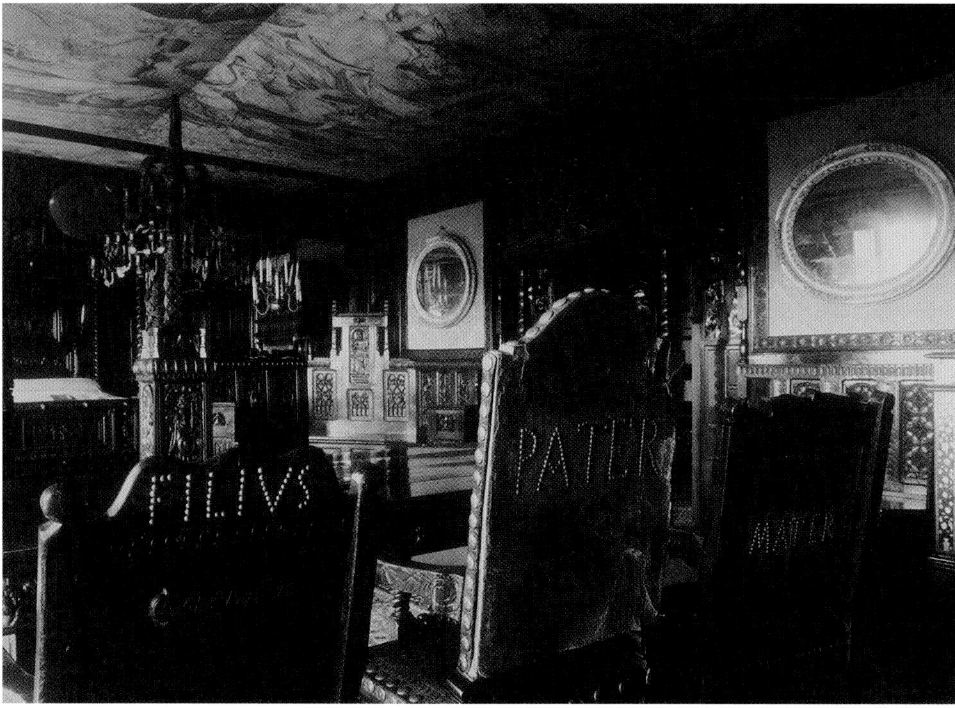

The 'workroom'

Victor Hugo designed the monumental candelabrum by the entrance to the study and named it *Tree of Fire*, probably after the Burning Bush. Rising almost to the ceiling, it is composed of sculpted panels representing the saints (Peter, Matthew, Paul and Andrew) and a candelabrum made from hollowed-out cotton reels, an idea Victor Hugo also used for the lighting of Hauteville Fairy. He took quite some time to compose the *Tree of Fire*, mentioning it in his diary from 4 January 1858 ('Today I gave Mauger the drawing for the large candelabrum. We traced it out') until 7 May 1859 ('The large wooden candelabrum which I call the *Tree of Fire* was finished today'). He modified the candelabrum in 1859, designing new elements separately: '21 [March] gave Mauger the orders and definitive drawing for the large candelabrum. I have given up the idea of a gas lamp. [...] 1 April I sculpted the folds behind the robe of the Virgin on the candelabrum. [...] 11 [April] I drew the branches of the wooden candelabrum.'

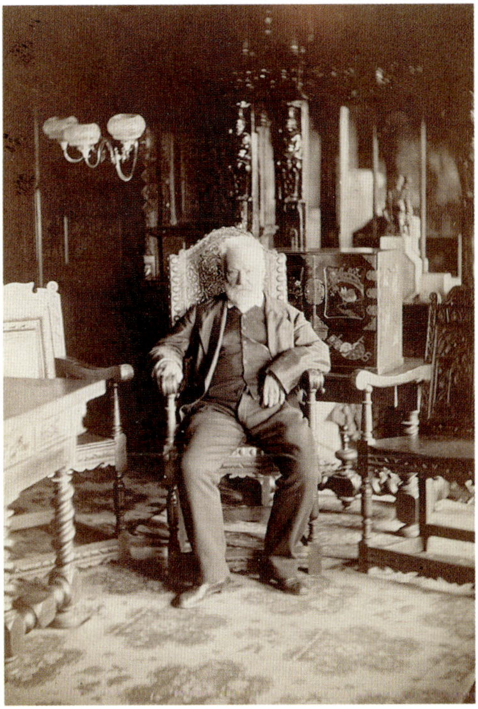

ill. 29
Joël Laiter
(born 1945)
The oak gallery, "Filius, Pater, Mater", 2001
Colour print on Toscana paper
26.6 x 39.5 cm
MVHP-PH-4395

ill. 30
André
Victor Hugo in the oak gallery, Hauteville House
Albumen print
14.5 x 10 cm
MVHP-PH-3395

Jean Biès saw the thirty-two branches as the symbol of the thirty-two 'Paths of Wisdom' of the Hebraic *Sepher Yetzirah*.[30]

The fireplace encased in a composition in wood at the end of the room recalls the one in the tapestries room. 'One is struck by the royal appearance of this fireplace; it could be the fireplace of Henri III,' Charles Hugo wrote to his mother on 14 March 1858. The large table in front of it, designed by Victor Hugo and made in November 1858, leaves little doubt as to why the room was known as the 'work room'. The three armchairs he placed at this table are in the same spirit as the 'ancestors' chair' in the dining room and contribute to the gallery's hieratic atmosphere. Initially called *PATER*, *FILIUS* and *SPIRITUS*, an allusion to the Holy Trinity, they finally became the more modest *PATER*, *FILIUS* and *MATER*, indicated by the inscriptions in brass studs on their leather backs.

30. Jean Biès, *op. cit.*, p. 146.

Victor Hugo wrote in his diary on 12 January 1859: 'The big leather armchair is finished. I wrote *PATER* behind it. I will write *FILIUS* behind the wooden armchair and *SPIRITUS* behind the medallion armchair. All three will be placed at the large table.' And on the 25 January: 'The third armchair is finished. Upon it I wrote *MATER*.' So the master of the house finally substituted the religion of the family for Christianity, and the worship of the father and patriarch for that of the Father.

Garibaldi's room

The workroom leads on into Victor Hugo's bedroom, called 'Garibaldi's room' from 1867, the year Garibaldi was defeated at Mentana. Garibaldi never came to Guernsey, however, despite the writer's repeated invitations.

In line with the armchairs, the *Tree of Fire* and the cabled columns, the gigantic canopied four-poster bed, composed of woodwork from various provenances, takes up the middle of the room. On 21 April 1859 the writer had *NOX MORS LUX* ('Night, death, light') engraved on its head. Our attention is immediately drawn to the whiteness of the small ivory sculpture at the top of the tiered bed head, con-

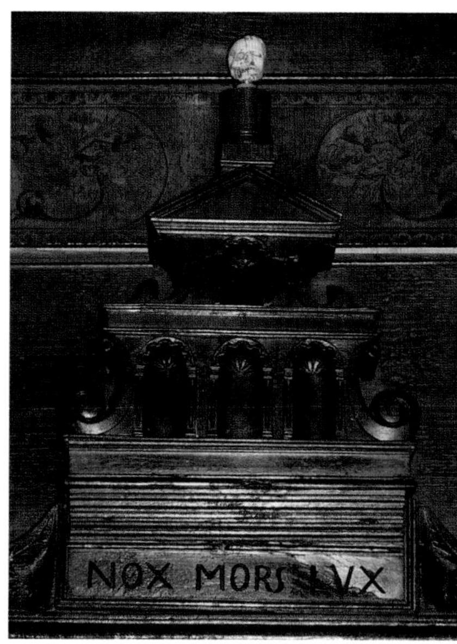

ill. 31
Detail of the head of the large bed in the Garibaldi room; tiered composition in oak with the inscription *NOX MORS LUX* ('night, death, light') on the base and the two-sided ivory head sculpted by James Pradier at the top

trasting with the dark wood below. The head has a man's face on one side and a skull on the other. It was sculpted by James Pradier, the father of Claire Pradier, Juliette Drouet's daughter, who was born in 1826 and died prematurely in 1846, at almost the same age as Léopoldine. Claire was very attached to Victor Hugo, who wrote her letters during her illness and dedicated one of the poems in *Contemplations* to her ('Claire', VI, December 1846). In 1859, Victor Hugo wrote in his third diary: '26 [September] Tom has installed the ivory bi-front (formerly the pommel of a walking stick) which Pradier gave me in 1843 on the pinnacle of the head of my large bed.' This *memento mori* transforms the bed into a funerary symbol.

The hypnotic gazes of many other heads echo the 'bi-front' in the oak gallery. As soon as one crosses the threshold one is met by small sculpted wooden heads, then again on the upper corners of the fireplace, on the corners of the large table and on the back of the stalls, while grotesques mingle with the mother-of-pearl and ivory-inlaid decoration of the Burgos wardrobe in the study.
This animation is reinforced by the many carved and painted inscriptions incorporated into the decoration, which literally make the room 'speak'. They include the Latin words *PERGE SURGE* ('Go forward, get up'), the two paradoxical formulae *SUM/ NON SEQUOR* ('I am' and 'I am not') and *STO/ SED FLEO* ('I am standing, but weeping'), engraved on the woodwork around the hearth, and the inscription *A DEO AD DEUM* ('From God to God') on the neo-gothic stalls. The entire gallery seems to be looking at us, talking to us.

The landing/library

'[...] As much as I like a book, I hate what the bourgeois calls a library.'
Victor Hugo, *Toute la lyre*, IV, 27

Deprived of the use of a public library on Guernsey, Victor Hugo had to compile one of his own, but chose not to devote a room to it and installed it on the landing. The 'landing/library' differs from traditional libraries of bourgeois houses, in which the book is a status symbol, decoration and a collector's item rather than something to be read.

The writer recorded many of his purchases in notebooks, and most of the books in the library have remained there [31]. Those acquired by Hugo are characteristically eclectic, ranging from anonymous works such as *The Cabinet of Enigmas, Gods, Goddesses and Heroes* (1680), to the *Holy Bible*, the *Koran*, the first edition of Diderot and Alembert's *Encyclopaedia*, and *The Delights of Great Britain and Ireland* (1859) by James Beeverell, which he referred to for *The Man Who Laughs*. He was also sent books from friends and acquaintances, like the two copies of *Les Chants de Maldoror* he received from Isidore Ducasse on 20 November 1868.

Shaped like a church nave or a boat, the landing/library acts as a transition space and the threshold of the more intimate realm of creation on the floor above. Victor Hugo, created a kind of spatial chiasm in the library using different light sources at the four cardinal points. The inscription in the shadows above the chiming clock reads:
'All leave their mark on both body and mind
All wound, alas – the last heals [32].'

31. See about the Jean-Bertrand Barrère's Library, *Victor Hugo à l'oeuvre*, « Les Livres de Hauteville House », Paris, Klincksieck, 1965.
32. It is a rewriting by Victor Hugo of the Latin proverb « Vulnerant omnes, ultima necat » (All hurt, the last kills.)

ill. 32
Georges Hugo
(1868–1925)
Victor Hugo coming down from the lookout at Hauteville House, circa 1878
Oil on canvas
45 x 37 cm
MVHP-P-268

ill. 33
Olivier Mériel
(born 1955)
Hauteville, landing/library, Friday 13 February 1998, 10 a.m.
Contact print
35.7 x 28.7 cm
MVHP-PH-2674

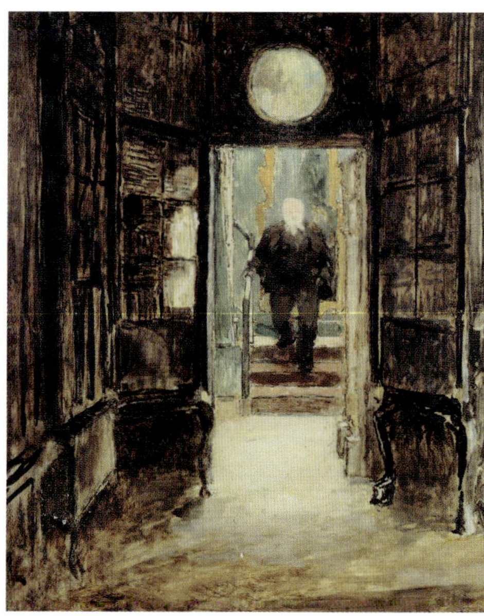

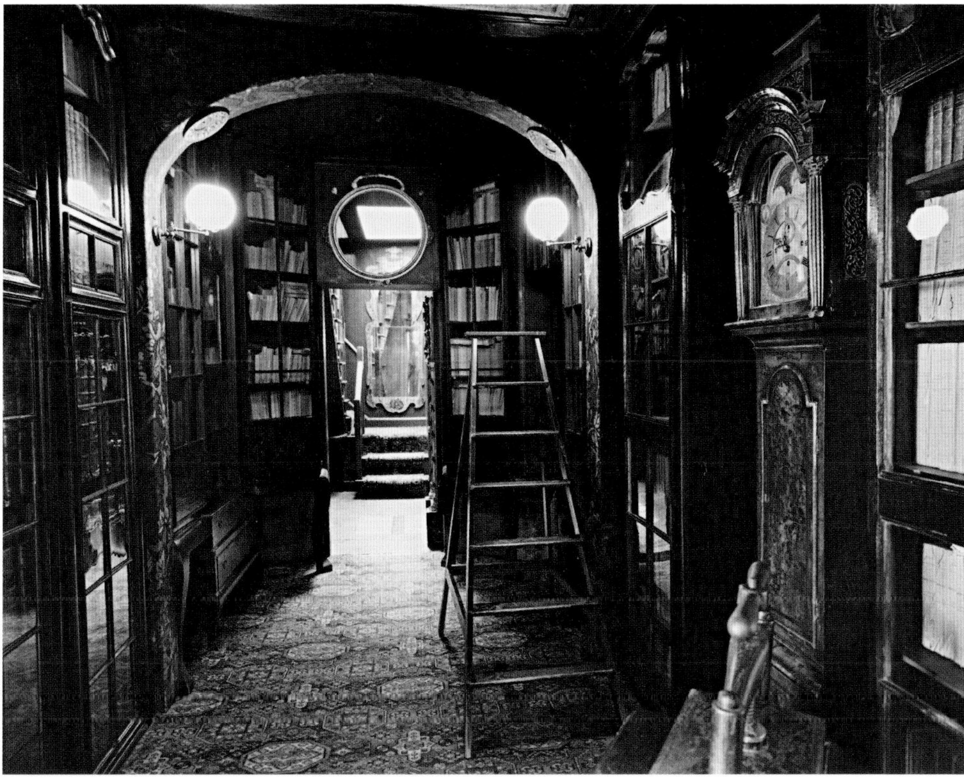

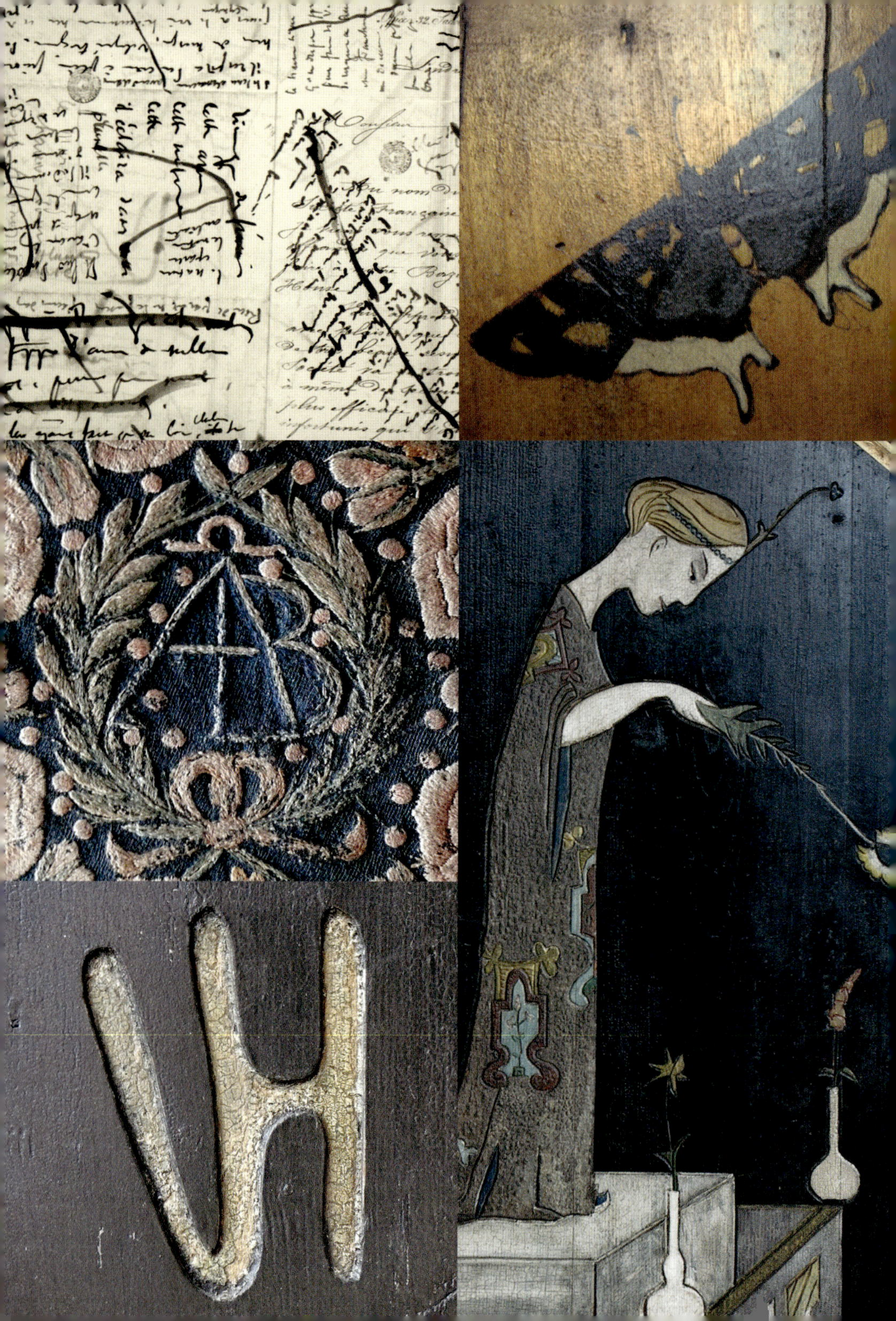

Third floor

The space narrows further and the climb towards the light becomes more tangible, materially expressing the Hugolian project of the preface to *The Legend of the Ages* (September 1859), to express mankind's every aspect, 'which can be summed up in a single, immense movement of ascension towards light'.

The antechamber

For a long time Victor Hugo used the antechamber to the lookout as a study, referring to it as the 'lookout' until the construction of the adjoining glazed room. Via a large window it gave onto a glazed cone rising from the staircase on the second floor and was always full of dazzling light. So even before the construction of the present lookout, in the now-famous letter he wrote to the young Belgian poet Franz Stevens on 10 April 1856, Victor Hugo described his workspace as a place opening onto a vista reflecting his own insularity: 'Do you realise my state of mind in the splendid solitude in which I am living, as though perched atop a rock, with all these great foaming waves and towering clouds at my window. I am living in the immense dream of the ocean, little by little I am becoming a sleepwalker of the sea [...]'. He wrote most of *The Legend of the Ages* on the 'small oak table with cabled legs' then in the room, which he gave to Juliette Drouet on 16 August 1859,[33] and which is now in place de Vosges. In the small library in the antechamber there are still the *Complete Works of William Shakespeare*, which François-Victor Hugo translated to have an activity during the exile, especially to earn his own income which would

33. Victor Hugo, 3rd diary, f° 35, 16 August 1859, Paris, BNF.

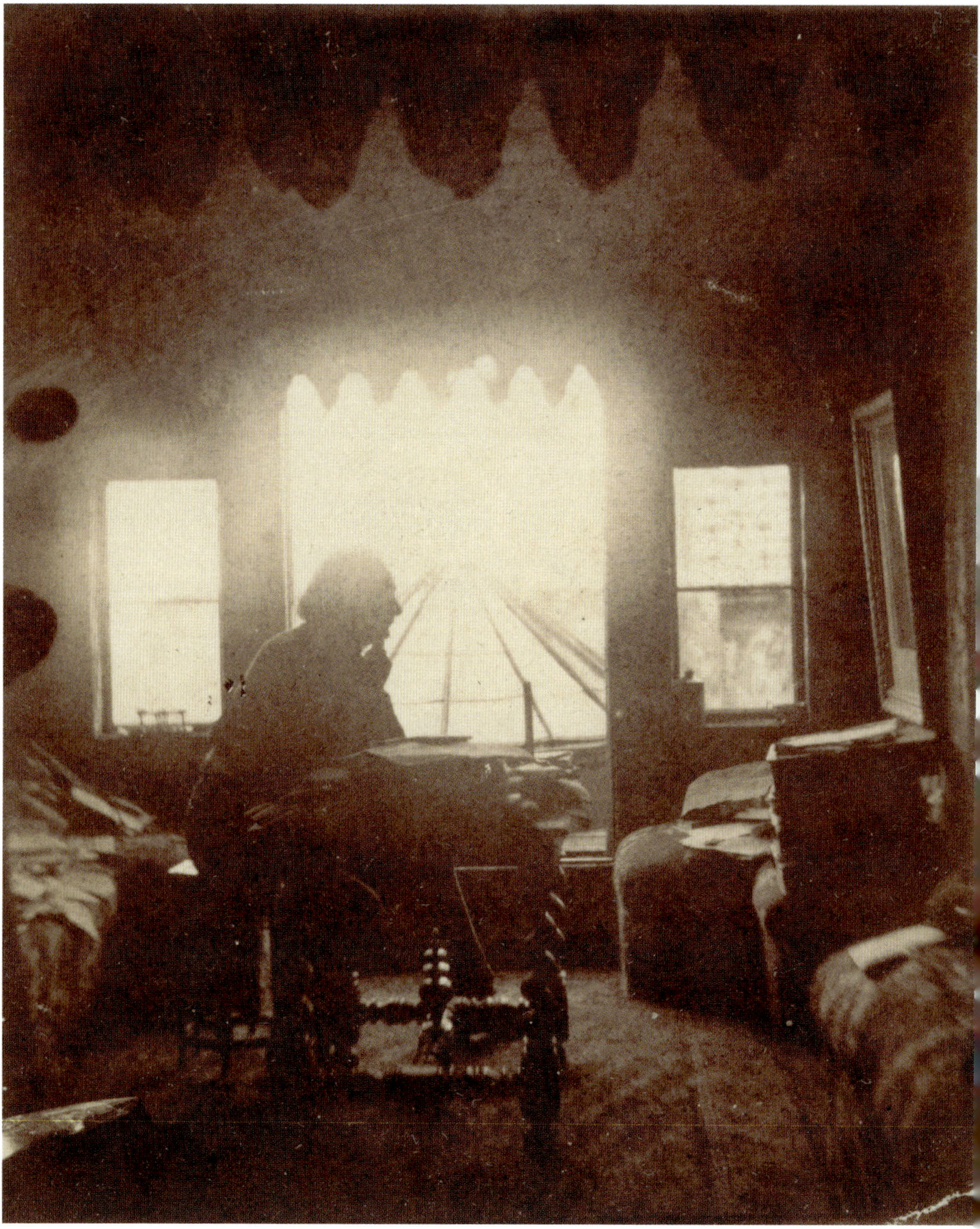

allow him to travel on the continent. His translation is still considered a standard reference work.
To the right of the door to the antechamber stands the piece of furniture called 'Anne Boleyn' because of the intertwined initials 'AB'. The fate of this queen from Shakespeare's time, executed by her husband, Henry VIII, symbolises the vanity of temporal power, eclipsed by the power of art. Victor Hugo drew the flowers inscribed in studs, and painted the insides of the drawers with floral plant motifs.

The lookout

'I am having a six square-metre Crystal Palace built on my roof. It will have a small fireplace and a table, with the sky and the ocean for seasoning.'

Victor Hugo to Auguste Vacquerie, 8 December 1861.

ill. 34
Anonymous
Victor Hugo in his workroom before the construction of the lookout, Hauteville House, between 1855 and 1861
Salt print
8.6 x 6.8 cm
MVHP-PH-1322 (1)

In October 1861, on his return from a trip to Belgium, Victor Hugo began the construction of a glass room on the roof, adjoining the study he called the 'crystal room' or 'lookout'. The dome lighting the main staircase was taken down and replaced by a large oval glass frame on the floor. On 2 April 1862, Victor Hugo wrote in his diary: 'I worked for the first time in the crystal room, even though it is far from finished.'
This room, technologically extremely modern for the time, contrasts with the rest of the house yet was conceived in the same spirit as the conservatory on the first floor and the 'lookout' in the garden behind the greenhouse (since demolished). Its steel and glass architecture transforms the link between house and nature, allowing the exterior to penetrate the interior: 'With glass architecture was born the first absolute space-light.'[34] From his lookout, the writer could take in Castle Cornet and Saint-Peter's Port at a glance, watch the construction of the new port and the harbour wall linking the castle and town, and could see the entire Channel Islands and, on a clear day, the Cotentin Peninsula.
Alone in this lookout, a spatial metaphor for creation and the solitary genius turned resolutely towards the future, Hugo worked at the hub of the universe, looking out over the sea and surrounded by sky.

34. Corinne Charles, *Victor Hugo. Visions d'intérieurs*, *op. cit.*, p. 60.

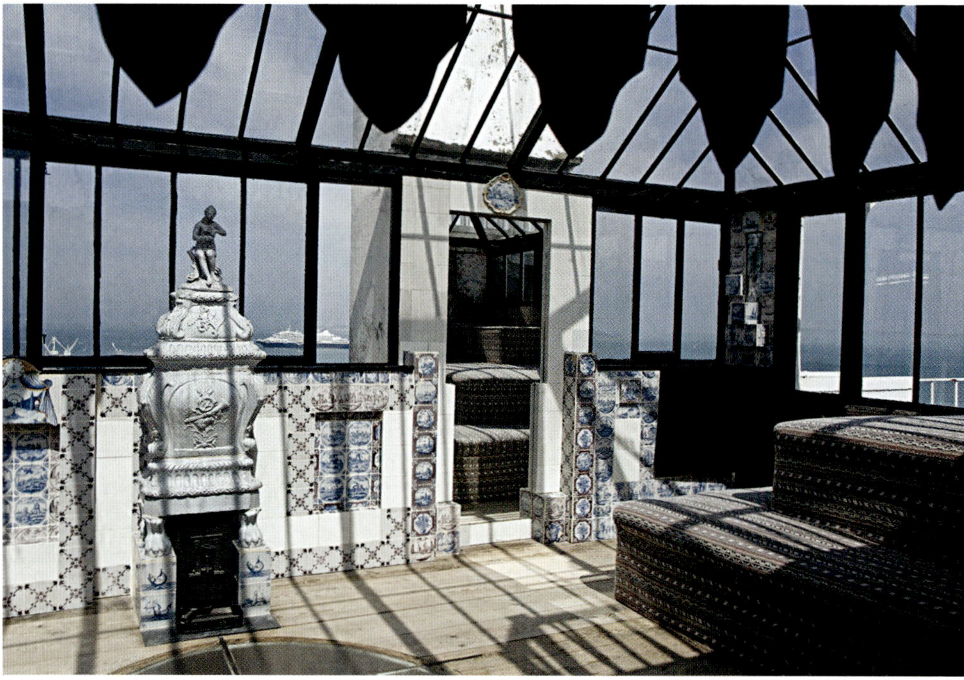

ill. 35
Hauteville House,
the lookout

The room's discreet decoration enhances the glass structure and increases the brilliance of the natural light tenfold. The gleaming violet, blue and white faience tiles echo the colours of the sea, while the three mirrors facing seaward reflect the port. The tiered seat covered with carpets, where the writer left his pages to dry, heightens the impression of ascension. The two key elements of its sober furnishings are the flapped wooden table at which Victor Hugo wrote standing before the infinite, and the glazed earthenware stove surmounted by a statue of Venus, which heated this often bitterly cold room. Georges Hugo recalled: 'He would enter the "lookout", the greenhouse on the roof, without blinds, in the midst of the burning blue sky reflected by the sea, and write, on a small tablet in front of a mirror he had decorated himself with a flower with strange petals and whose silvering had bubbled and crackled in the heat.'[35]

35. Georges Hugo, *Mon grand-père*, *op. cit.*, p. 36.

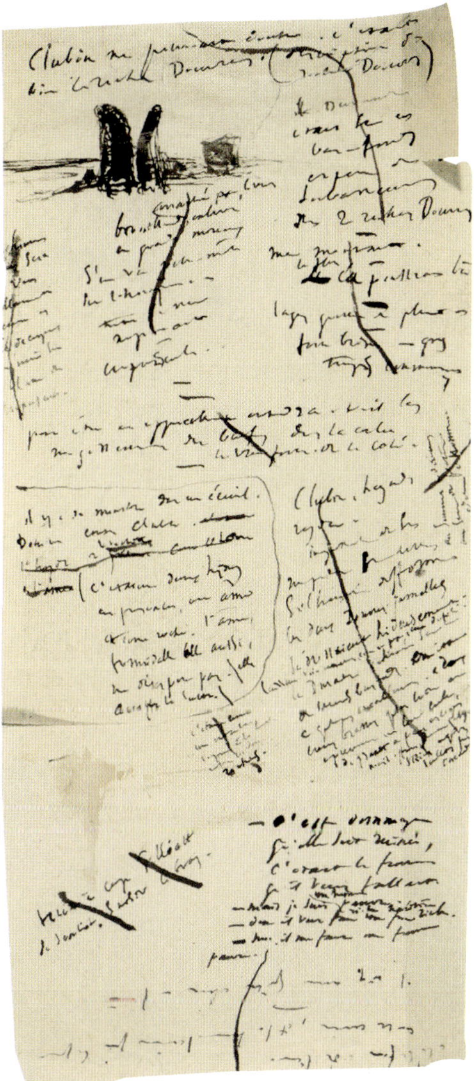

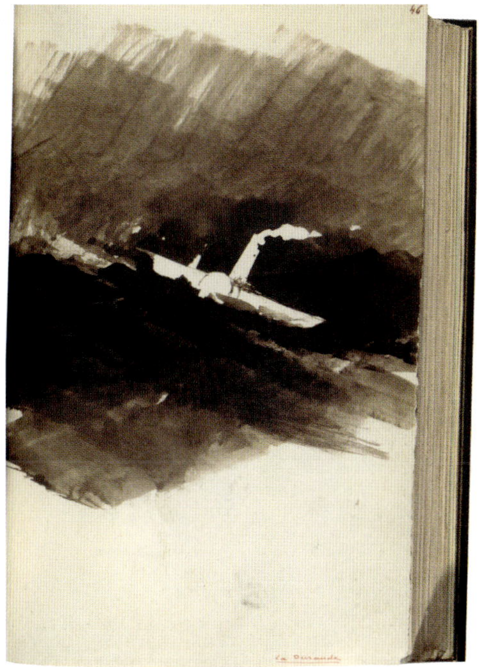

ill. 36
Victor Hugo
(1802–85)
Untitlcd, 1861 66
Pon and brown ink on vellum paper
33 x 14.5 cm
MVHP-L-9817 (10)

ill. 37
Victor Hugo
(1802–85)
La Durando, 1861 66?
Pen, brush or feather brush and brown ink wash on vellum paper
22.7 x 14 cm
MVHP-L-9817 (46)

Mounted at the beginning of Victor Hugo's copy of tho firct odition of *The Toilers of the Sea* (Brussels, A. Lacroix and Verboeckhoven, 1866) vol. I

Here, 'Writing returns to the book and the house hushes to let the work speak'.[36] It was in the lookout and the antechamber, Hauteville House's 'cockpit', the 'fulcrum on which converged the cardinal breaths of creation and inspiration',[37] the 'glasshouse' where the alchemist's 'work was carried out',[38] that Victor Hugo conceived and wrote many of his works. It was here that he wrote the end of *Les Misérables* (1862), *William Shakespeare* (1864), *Songs of the Street and the Wood* (1865), *The Toilers of the Sea*, *One Thousand Franc Reward*, *The Intervention*, *Will They Eat?* (1867), *The Man Who Laughs*, *The Sword*, and *Torquemada* (1869). It was also here that he began *Ninety-Three*, on his return to Guernsey in 1872–73, and wrote thousands of verses for *The Art of Being a Grandfather*, *The Four Winds of the Spirit*, *The Fateful Years*, *The Whole Lyre*, *Last Gleanings* and *Free Theatre*.

From dawn to midday he worked in this 'little glazed belvedere encompassing every horizon, enormous for the soul, cramped for the body, containing everything in a tiny space like a sea captain's cabin.[39]'

When he returned to Hauteville House from Paris after his exile, Victor Hugo appreciated its calm and the solitude it afforded him to write. He confided to Auguste Vacquerie on 3 January 1873: 'What roots me here is the necessity to not leave this life without having done my whole duty and completed my work as far as possible. A month's work here is worth a year in Paris. This is why I sentence myself to exile.'

Victor Hugo's bedroom

Georges Hugo remembers his grandfather's bedroom as a 'kind of niche in the attic': small and quite bare, with a large glazed bay looking out on the sky and the ocean, it does indeed remind one of a sea captain's cabin. From this room, which he also called his 'lookout', the writer could see La Fallue, the house Juliette Drouet lived in until 1864. He spent many a sleepless night in this bedroom, prey to hallucinations and 'knockings', and eventually moved into his son

36. Chantal Brière, *Victor Hugo et le roman architectural*, *op. cit.*, p. 556.
37. Jean Biès, *op. cit.*, p. 142.
38. *Ibid.*, p. 149.
39. Charles Hugo, *Chez Victor Hugo par un passant*, *op. cit.*, p. 64.

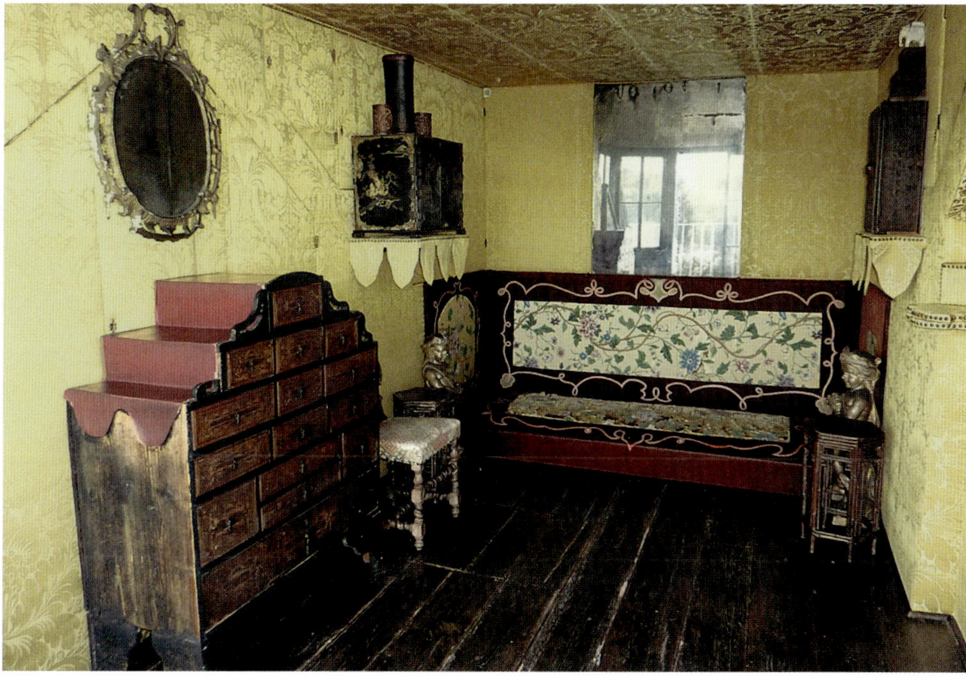

ill. 38
Hauteville House, Victor Hugo's bedroom

François-Victor's bedroom on the other side of the oak gallery after he left Guernsey for good in 1865.[40]

The room contains several references to childhood: two portraits of Léopoldine, two gilt terracotta figurines of children, an elephant (associated with Gavroche since *Les Misérables*) and two pyrographed wood panels whose narrative fascinated the writer/interior designer's grandchildren. Georges Hugo recounted: 'Two wooden panels sculpted and painted by him, conceal his washstand on one side and a wardrobe on the other. The story of a beauty, a knight and a beast. We were so intrigued by these drawings that we sometimes took Papapa up to this room to tell it to us. And he would recount how the knight, who loved the damsel, had to kill the dragon and bring her its head to win her love. Adding words to the drawing, he would describe the combat between the knight and the monster with hooked claws, whose ringed tail twisted with rage; how the

40. Victor Hugo, 6th diary, 19 February 1865, Paris, BNF: 'My nights are too troubled by this singular obsession, I have decided to go and sleep in Victor's bedroom.'

damsel's suitor, riding a fantastic bird, slew the dragon with a single thrust of his lance down its throat. [...] the flower the damsel was holding with the gesture of a little idol was the symbol of the pure love she gave to her lover.'[41]
Victor Hugo wrote in his dairy on 10 March 1864: 'I drew yesterday and today the two large panels with the dragon for my lookout.' Borrowing the iconography of Saint George slaying the dragon, which also inspired the flapped table he made for Juliette Drouet in 1857, the panels are decorated in the same style as those in the Chinese drawing room he designed for his mistress's second house on

41. Georges Hugo, *Mon grand-père*, *op. cit.*, p. 36–37.

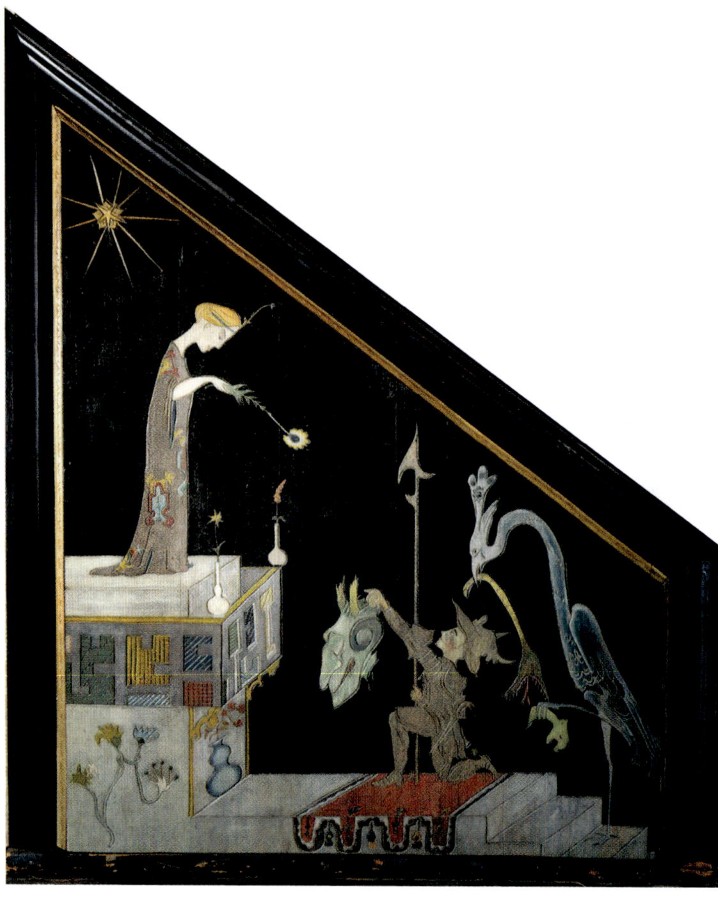

Guernsey, Hauteville Fairy. The table and panels are now in place des Vosges in Paris. Although the iconography is medieval, its representation is influenced by Japonism: the dragon's head evokes a mask and the princess's dress resembles a kimono. Victor Hugo's use of empty space in the scene showing the combat between the crane and the dragon has similarities with the Japanese woodblock prints that began reaching London and Paris in the mid-19th century. The panels lower to reveal a small cupboard and the writer's toiletries. Every morning, he subjected himself to his cold water 'hydrotherapy' on the roof, like some purifying and revitalising ritual bath.

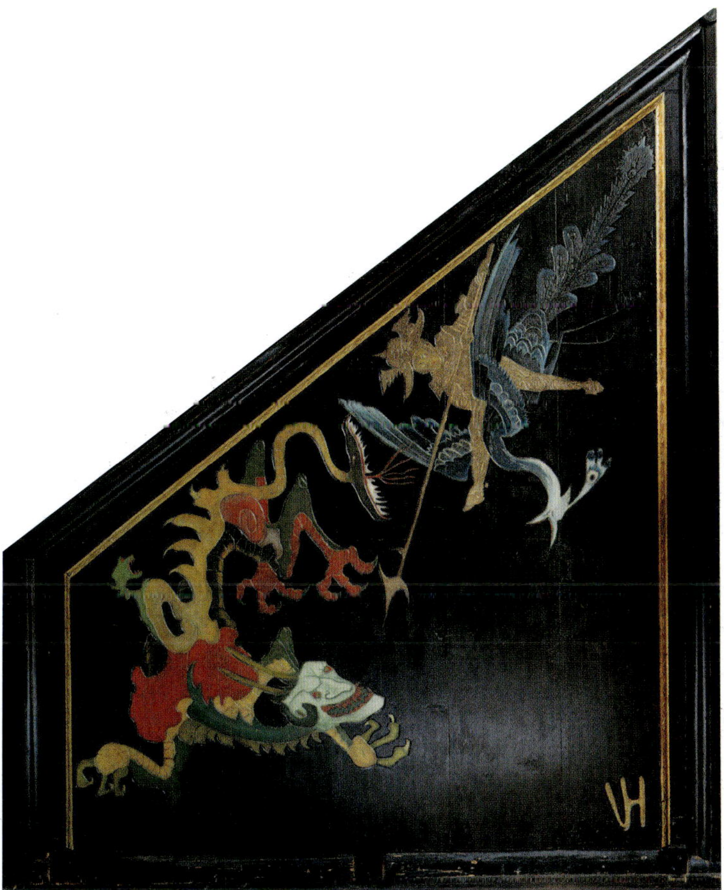

ill. 39
Panels in Victor Hugo's bedroom
Wood pyrographed and painted by Victor Hugo
2 quadrilaterals with the same dimensions: 162.6 x 134 x 59.5 x 169.5 cm
(thickness: 5 cm)

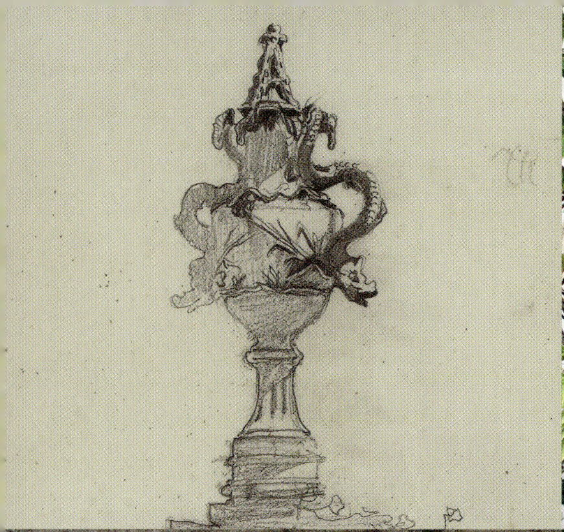
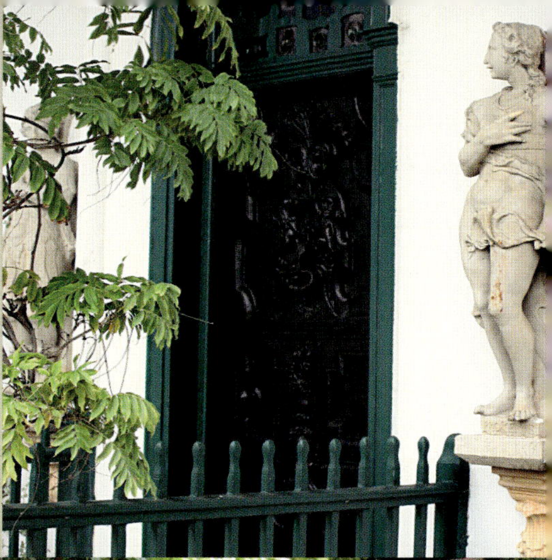
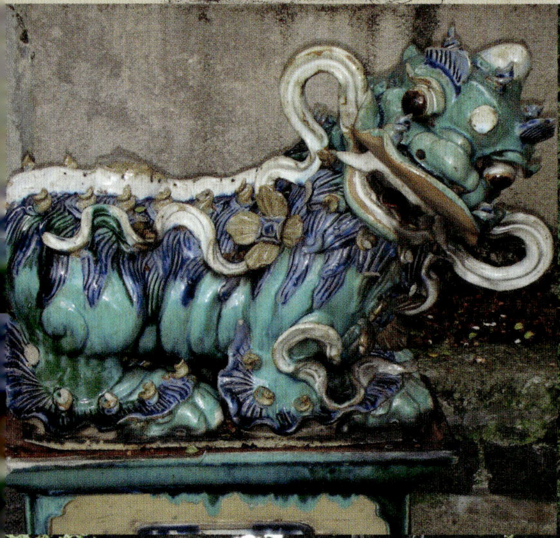
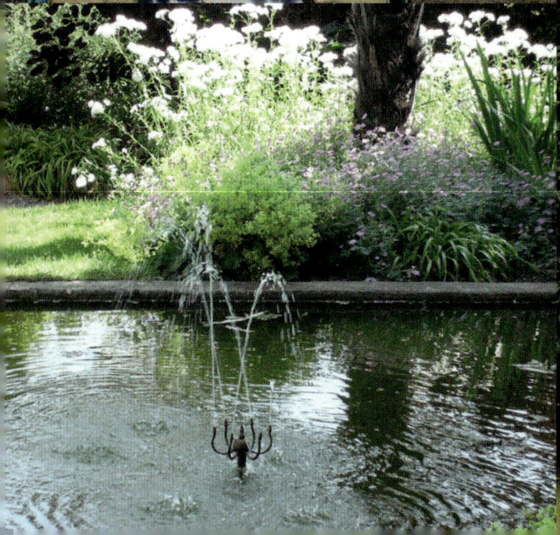
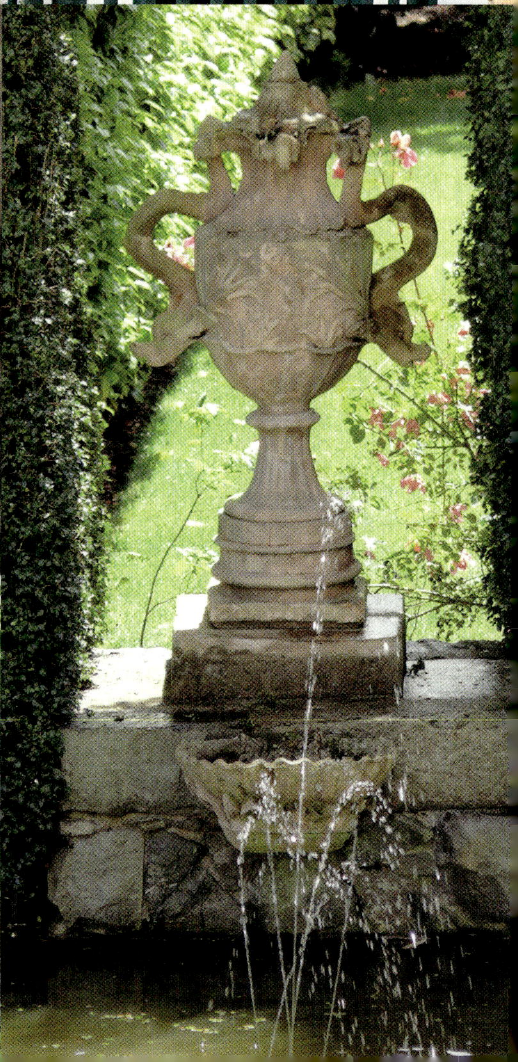

The garden

Hauteville House's garden, laid out from 1856, was restored in 2002 for the bicentenary of Victor Hugo's birth, following the indications in his diaries. Visitors can now enjoy the trees and plants which grew there during Victor Hugo's time. Like the unnamed God of *The Archipelago of the Channel*, he imagined his garden like 'a rather dreamy entomologist' and 'somewhat naturalist poet',[42] taking advantage of Guernsey's mild climate, which enabled him to grow lavender, rhododendrons, fuchsias, lilies, carnations, resedas, azaleas, wisteria, myrtle, and also aloes, fig trees, rushes and lilac. A eucalyptus tree planted by the writer in 1870 is still standing.

From the terrace outside the smoking room slightly overhanging the garden, stretches a lawn dominated by a stone fountain with two snake-shaped handles, known as the 'snake fountain'. It is reflected in the large pond, which Victor Hugo had stocked with goldfish. ('3 June 1857 four goldfish for the pond'). Purchased by the writer in August 1847, it was previously in the garden of the Hugo's apartment in place Royale. The plinth bears the inscription *UBI SPES IBI PAX* ('Where there is hope there is peace') and the date, *17 October 1856 V.H.* Victor Hugo drew it in 1857, inverting the habitual process of first drawing objects and then having them made. The pond and fountain are mentioned in the poem *My Garden* (*Last Gleanings*, XVIII):

'The basin gleams in the grass and beneath the sky
Seems like a crystal mirror bordered with green felt;
[…]

42. *The Archipelago of the Channel*, chap. IV, 'L'Herbe'.

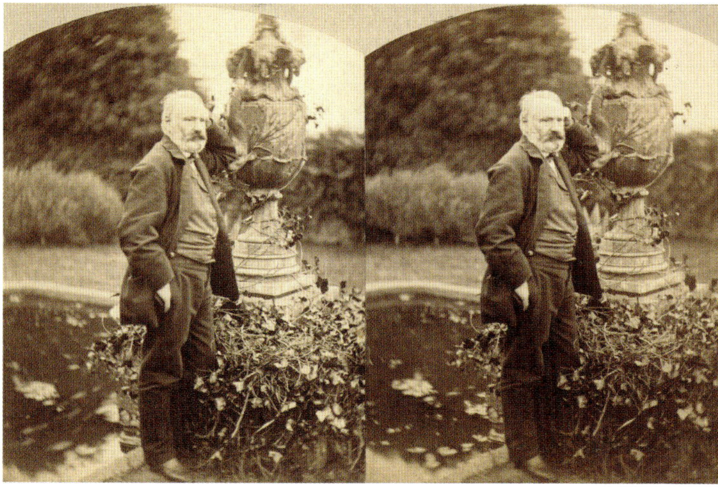

ill. 40
Edmond Bacot
(1814–75)
Victor Hugo in front of the fountain, Hauteville House, stereoscopic view, 1862
Albumen print
8.5 x 6.3 cm
MVHP-PH-1321 (5)

And, bric-a-brac from Anet and Versailles,
Taken from the den of some nymph Echo,
A terracotta vase in the rococo style,
In the water that trembles with confused cadences,
Mirrors the two snakes acting as its handles.'

The Chinese glazed earthenware Fu dogs and dragon's heads act as temple guardians. Victor Hugo had these lines from *Contemplations* engraved on the right-hand wall: *Immensity! said the Being. Eternity! said the Soul* ('Magnitudo Parvi'). The stone bench against the wall evokes the one on which Marius and Cosette sat together in the garden in rue Plumet in *Les Misérables*. In front of this wall one discovers a second lawn, framed by a camellia hedge, and on the other side, a greenhouse. There was originally another greenhouse, used for growing grapes, where from 1859 the family lunched during the summer months and enjoyed its wine. An aviary for canaries and Australian birds was installed in 1857. A vegetable garden was tended by the gardener, Henri (or Henry), where he grew potatoes, peas, beans, asparagus, rhubarb and strawberries.

A tree could be said to be the garden's main character: the oak of the United States of Europe, planted by Victor Hugo on 14 July 1870. He wrote in his diary: 'Today, 14 July 1870, at one o'clock in the afternoon, my gardener Tourtell assisting me, in the company of my son Charles, [...] and Mme Charles Hugo, [...] Chenay, and with little Georges and little Jeanne present, I planted in my garden the acorn from which will grow the oak I am baptising *Oak of the United States of Europe.*' He glued a portrait of Georges next to this text, concretising the parallelism between the tree, his descendents and the future: 'Opposite this page I am putting the portrait of little Georges who, I hope, D.V [*Deo Volente*], will see the twentieth century.' He devoted a poem to the Hauteville House oak in *The Four Winds of the Spirit*, 'As I Planted the Oak of the United States of Europe' (21 July 1870):

'Let us sow that which remains,
O passers-by that we are!
Fate is an abyss, its waters bitter,
On the brink of black destiny, brothers, let us sow men,
And oaks beside the seas!
[...]
There is an oak of the Republic within us all;
There is an oak of Truth with us all;'

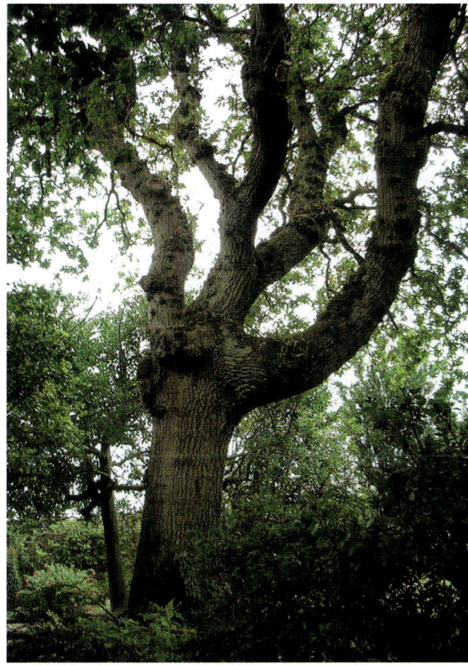

ill. 41
Hauteville House, the garden, the oak of the United States of Europe

The oak, a republican symbol rooted in the collective psyche, is here above all a metaphor for the 'true poet' who cannot be imitated: 'The true poet is a tree that can be lashed by all winds and showers, who carries his works like his fruit' (preface to *Cromwell*). In the Guernsey garden, the oak is primarily a self-portrait or *alter ego* of the master of the house, of the visionary and rebel genius: 'The oak, that giant tree which we were comparing to Shakespeare just now, and which has more than one point of resemblance to him, the oak that has an unusual shape, gnarled branches, dark leaves and hard, rough bark; but is the oak. And it is because of this that he is the oak. If you would have a smooth trunk, straight branches, satiny leaves, apply to the pale birch, the hollow elder, the weeping willow; but leave the mighty oak in peace.' (preface to *Cromwell*)
After his return to France, the tree embodied the poet's continual spiritual presence at Hauteville House: 'The oak [...] sprung from the earth on 5 September, the day of my return to Paris,' Hugo wrote in his diary on 13 September 1870.

ill. 42
Arsène Garnier
(1822–1900)
Victor Hugo in the garden, Hauteville House, 1868
Albumen print
10.8 x 7.2 cm
MVHP-PH-4357

Victor Hugo conceived Hauteville House as he wrote his books, isolating fragments of objects to integrate them into new compositions, reusing them as formal metaphors, using digressions to create unity, drawing sustenance from anything he could find, like a veritable 'Gargantua of the beautiful' (*Postscript to My Life*). One could say of this house what Yves Gohin said about *The Toilers of the Sea*, that it is 'a novel of totality, a novel of solitude'.[43] Hauteville House is both the 'residence of totality' where Hugo brought together the senses and thought, concretising his aspiration for unity in everything, his quest for light and faith in the power of art and human perfectibility, and the 'residence of solitude' in which the creator saw its other occupants leave one by one to lead their own lives. Both refuge and ruin, it was a sanctuary built by a poet to ward off exile and death. Victor Hugo made Hauteville House into a microcosm of the infinite, a residence which is 'in space what the dream is in time: the aquarium of the night'.[44] And his presence is still palpable.

Leïla Jarbouai

43. Yves Gohin, preface to *Les Travailleurs de la mer* (Paris, Gallimard, 1980) p. 8.
44. *Ibid.*, p. 17.

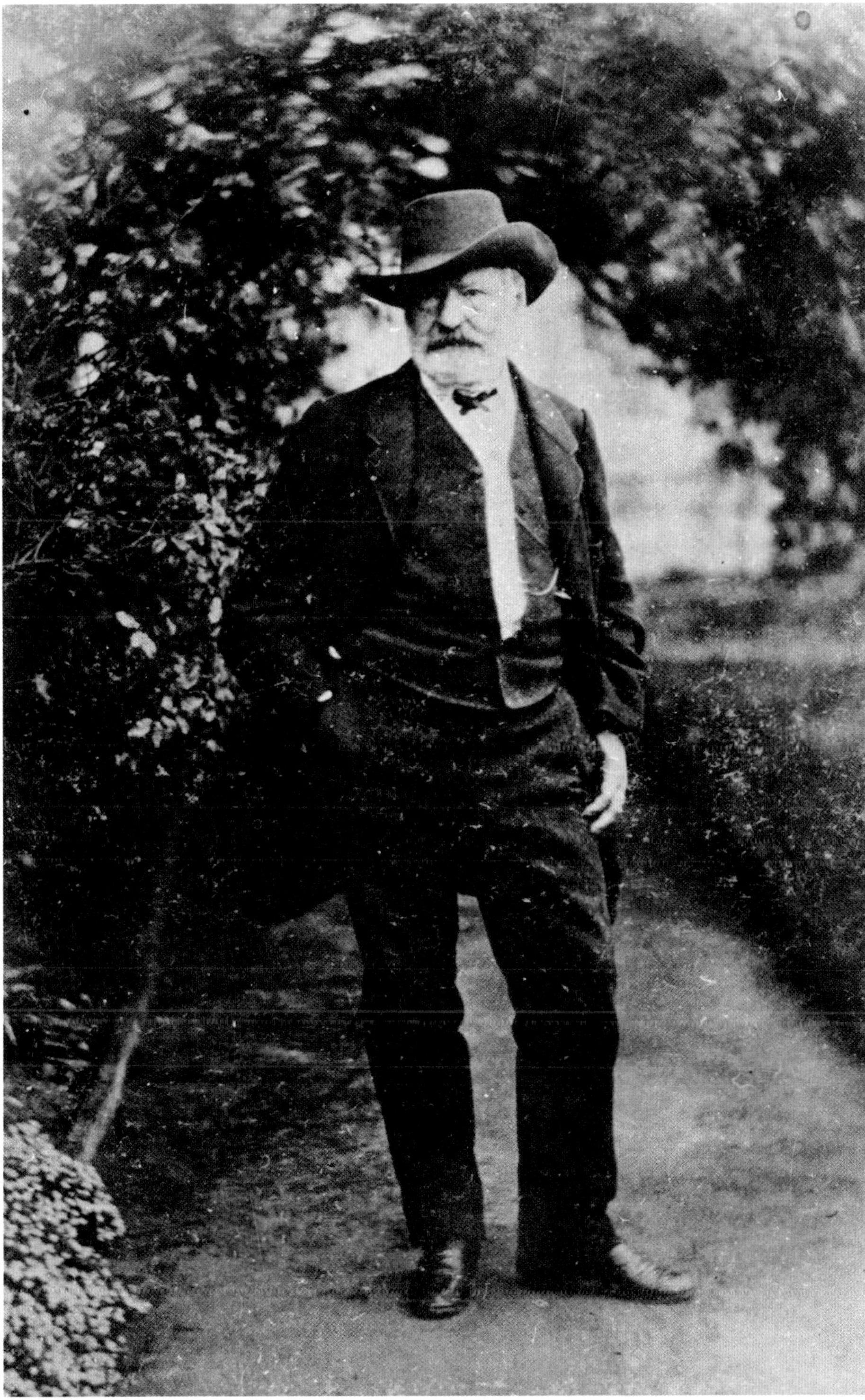

Learn more

Victor Hugo's Works

Victor Hugo. Œuvres complètes, edited by Jean Massin, Paris, Club français du livre, 18 vol., 1966-1970.

Victor Hugo. Œuvres complètes, edited by Jacques Seebacher, Guy Rosa, le Groupe Hugo, Paris, Robert Laffont, 2002.

General works

ADÈLE HUGO, *Victor Hugo raconté par un témoin de sa vie*, Paris, Librairie internationale A. Lacroix, Verboeckhoven & Cie, 1863.

CHARLES HUGO, *Chez Victor Hugo par un passant*, illustrated by twelve etchings by Maxime Lalanne, Paris, Cadart et Luquet, 1864.

JULES CLARETIE, *Victor Hugo*, Paris, 1882.

HENRI HOUSSAYE, *De Marine Terrace à Hauteville House*, articles, *Journal des débats*, 15 and 18 September 1885.

GUSTAVE LARROUMET, *La Maison de Victor Hugo. Impressions guernesiaises*, Paris, Honoré Champion, 1895.

PAUL CHENAY, *Victor Hugo à Guernesey. Souvenirs de son beau-frère*, Paris, Félix Juven, 1902.

JULES CLARETIE, *Victor Hugo. Souvenirs intimes*, Paris, L. Maretheux, 1902.

GEORGES HUGO, *Mon grand-père*, Paris, Calmann-Lévy, 1902.

GUSTAVE SIMON, *La Vie d'une femme*, Paris, Ollendorff, 1914, p. 311-387.

RENÉ WEISS, *La Maison de Victor Hugo à Guernesey (Hauteville-House) propriété de la Ville de Paris*, Paris, Imprimerie nationale, 1928.

JEAN DELALANDE, *Victor Hugo à Hauteville House*, Paris, Albin Michel, 1947.

JEAN-BERTRAND BARRÈRE, *Victor Hugo à l'œuvre. Le poète en exil et en voyage*, Paris, Klincksieck, 1965.

MARTINE ÉCALLE, *Perles et broderies chez Victor Hugo*, Ville de Paris, Maisons de Victor Hugo, 1973.

ROBERT SABOURIN, *Hauteville House, Maison de Victor Hugo*, Rennes, Ouest-France, 1983.

ANNETTE BROCK, *Hauteville House, maison d'exil de Victor Hugo*, Paris, Musées de la Ville de Paris, 1984.

JEAN BIÈS, 'Hauteville House ou le caravansérail de la rêverie', *Europe*, n° 671, March 1985.

HENRI CAZAUMAYOU, *Maison de Victor Hugo, Dessins de Victor Hugo*, notes collated by Sophie Grossiord and *alii*, Paris, Paris-Musées, 1985.

GÉRARD POUCHAIN, *Promenades dans l'archipel de la Manche avec un guide*, Condé-sur-Noireau, Éditions Charles Corlet, 1985-2002.

SOPHIE GROSSIORD, *Hauteville House. Guide général*, Paris, Paris-Musées, 1993.

CORINNE CHARLES, 'Moyen Âge et romantisme : le mobilier de Victor Hugo', *Revue suisse d'art et d'archéologie*, Zurich, Schwegler, 1997, vol. 54, n° 2, p. 197-205.

SOPHIE GROSSIORD, *Victor Hugo, et s'il n'en reste qu'un...*, Paris, Découvertes Gallimard / Paris-Musées, 1998.

Joël Laiter, *Victor Hugo, l'exil. L'Archipel de la Manche*, Paris, Hazan, 2001.

Jean-Marc Hovasse, *Victor Hugo*, t. I : *Avant l'exil, 1802-1851*, Paris, Fayard, 2001 ; t. II : *Pendant l'exil, 1851-1864*, Paris, Fayard, 2008.

Corinne Charles, *Victor Hugo, visions d'intérieurs, du meuble au décor*, bilingual French/English, Paris, Paris-Musées, 2003.

Chantal Brière, *Victor Hugo et le roman architectural*, Paris, Honoré Champion, 2007.

Maison de Victor Hugo Museum Guide, edited by Danielle Molinari, Paris. Paris-Musées, 2009.

Gérard Pouchain, *Dans les pas de Victor Hugo en Normandie et aux îles anglo-normandes*, Cully, Éditions Orep, 2010.

Danielle Molinari, *Victor Hugo, visions graphiques*, Paris. Paris-Musées. 'Petites Capitales', 2010.

Exhibition catalogues

Soleil d'encre. Manuscrits et dessins de Victor Hugo, edited by Judith Petit, Roger Pierrot and Marie-Laure Prévost, Paris, BNF, Paris, Paris-Musées, 1985.

En collaboration avec le soleil. Victor Hugo, photographies de l'exil, edited by Françoise Heilbrun and Danielle Molinari, Paris, musée d'Orsay and Maison de Victor Hugo, Paris, RMN / Paris-Musées, 1998.

Dans l'intimité de Victor Hugo à Hauteville House, Olivier Mériel, 1998. Photographies, Paris, Maison de Victor Hugo, Paris, Paris-Musées, 1998-1999.

Du chaos dans le pinceau, Madrid, musée Thyssen-Bornemisza, Paris, Maison de Victor Hugo, Paris, Paris-Musées, 2000-2001.

Exilium Vita Est. Victor Hugo à Guernesey, Guernesey, Hauteville House, Paris, Paris-Musées, 2002.

Victor Hugo, l'homme océan, edited by Marie-Laure Prévost, Paris, BNF, Paris, BNF/Seuil, 2002.

Timeline

Before exile

1802 Birth of Victor Hugo at Besançon (26 February).
1821 Death of Victor Hugo's mother, Sophie Hugo, born Trébuchet.
1822 *Odes et poésies diverses*. Victor Hugo marries Adèle Foucher.
1823 *Han d'Islande*. Birth and death of Victor and Adèle Hugo's son Léopold-Victor.
1824 Birth of their daughter Léopoldine.
1825 *Nouvelles Odes*. Awarded the Légion d'honneur. Goes to Reims for the coronation of Charles X. Travels to the Alps.
1826 Birth of Charles Hugo. *Odes et ballades*.
1827 Publication of *Cromwell* and its famous preface.
1828 Death of General Hugo. Birth of Victor, known as François-Victor Hugo.
1829 *Orientalia*, *Le Dernier Jour d'un condamné*. The play *Marion Delorme* is banned.
1830 *Hernani*. Birth of Adèle Hugo. July Revolution and ascension of the liberal monarch Louis-Philippe.
1831 *Notre-Dame de Paris*. First performance and publication of *Marion Delorme*. *Autumn Leaves*.
1832 *Le Roi s'amuse* is banned after the first performance.
1833 *Lucrèce Borgia*. Beginning of his relationship with Juliette Drouet. *Marie Tudor*.
1834 *Littérature et philosophie mêlées*, *Claude Gueux*. First travels with Juliette Drouet.
1835 *Angelo, tyran de Padoue*, *Les Chants du crépuscule*.
1837 Death of his brother Eugène. *Les Voix intérieures*.
1838 *Ruy Blas*.
1839 Visits Alsace, Switzerland, Provence and Burgundy with Juliette Drouet.
1840 Trip to the Rhineland with Juliette Drouet. *Sunlight and Shadows*.
1841 Elected to the Académie française (after four attempts).
1842 *The Rhine*.
1843 Léopoldine marries Charles Vacquerie. The newlyweds drown in the Seine (4 September). *Les Burgraves*.
1845 Appointed a peer of France. His affair with Léonie Biard causes a scandal. Begins writing *Les Misères*, (*Les Misérables*).
1848 Proclamation of the French Republic. Elected deputy for Paris at the National Constituent Assembly. Speech defending the liberty of the press. His son founds the newspaper *L'Événement* with Paul Meurice and Auguste Vacquerie.
1849 Elected deputy for Paris at the Legislative Assembly. Speech on poverty. President of the International Peace Congress.
1850 Speech defending freedom of education and universal suffrage.

During exile

1851 Opposes Louis-Napoléon Bonaparte's coup d'état. Sought by the police, flees France for Brussels.
1852 *Napoléon-le-Petit*. Auction of his furniture in Paris. Moves to Jersey (Marine Terrace).
1853 The Hugo family initiated to table-turning by Delphine de Girardin. Photographic workshop. Clandestine publication of *Châtiments*.
1854 *Aux habitants de Guernesey*, *Lettre à Lord Palmerston* against the execution of Tapner,

Les Discours de l'exil. Writes parts of *La Fin de Satan* (published in 1886).

1855 *Discours pour les États-Unis d'Europe*. Writes part of *Dieu* (published in 1896). Expelled from Jersey. Moves to Guernsey (31 October), into 20 Hauteville Street. Death of his brother Abel.

1856 *Contemplations*. Buys Hauteville House (38 Hauteville Street) on 16 May. The family moves in on 17 October.

1857 Visited by Alexandre Dumas. House warming party (14 May).

1859 Refuses the amnesty offered to exiles by Napoleon III. First series of *The Legend of the Ages*. Text and drawing in defence of John Brown, hung in the United States. Works on *Songs of the Street and the Wood*, *The Legend of the Ages*, *Torquemada* and *La Fin de Satan*.

1860 Visits Jersey.

1861 Travels in Belgium and Holland. Builds the lookout on the roof of Hauteville House.

1862 Publication of *Les Misérables* in Brussels and Paris. First dinner for poor children. Trip to Belgium, Luxembourg and the Rhine. Edmond Bacot photographs Hauteville House.

1863 Adèle Hugo joins her lover, Lieutenant Pinson, in Canada. Mme Hugo writes *Victor Hugo raconté par un témoin de sa vie*. Travels in Belgium and Germany with Juliette Drouet.

1864 Mme Hugo now divides her time between Paris and Brussels. *William Shakespeare*. Trip to the Ardennes and the Rhineland. Juliette Drouet moves into 20 Hauteville Street.

1865 *Songs of the Street and the Wood*. Stays in Brussels and Germany. Charles Hugo marries Alice Lehaene. Mme Hugo moves to Brussels.

1866 Stays in Brussels. *The Toilers of the Sea*, *One Thousand Franc Reward*, *The Intervention*.

1867 Trip to Zeeland. *Lettre à Juarez*, *La Voix de Guernesey*, *Will They Eat?* New production of *Hernani* at the Théâtre-Français.

1868 Performance of *Hernani* on Guernesey. Birth of Charles' son Georges. Death of Mme Hugo.

1869 *The Man Who Laughs*. Birth of Charles' daughter Jeanne. Victor Hugo's son founds the newspaper *Le Rappel* with Paul Meurice, Auguste Vacquerie and Henri Rochefort. President of the Peace congress at Lausanne.

1870 Plants the oak of the United States of Europe in the garden at Hauteville House. Returns to France on 4 September, after the proclamation of the 3rd Republic.

After exile

1871 Elected deputy for Paris, attends the National Assembly in Bordeaux but soon resigns. Death of Charles. Offers asylum for the communards in Brussels. Expelled from Belgium, leaves for Luxembourg (Vianden).

1872 *L'Année terrible*. Internment of his daughter Adèle. Stays a year on Guernsey.

1873 Returns to Paris. Death of François-Victor.

1874 *Ninety-Three*.

1875 *Actes et paroles*, volumes I and II (*Avant l'exil* and *Pendant l'exil*), *Mes fils*. Stays on Guernsey for a week.

1876	Elected a senator, proposes amnesty for the communards. Pursues his struggle against the death penalty. *Actes et paroles*, volume III (Depuis l'exil).
1877	*Histoire d'un crime*, *The Art of Being a Grandfather*. *The Legend of the Ages*, new series.
1878	Stays four months on Guernsey (August–November).
1881	Celebrates his 80th birthday.
1882	*Torquemada*.
1883	Death of Juliette Drouet. *The Archipelago of the Channel.*
1885	Death of Victor Hugo (22 May). State funeral (1 June).
1903	Inauguration of the Maison de Victor Hugo, place des Vosges, Paris.
1915	Death of Adèle Hugo.
1927	The writer's descendents donate Hauteville House to the City of Paris.

Practical Information

Hauteville House

38 Hauteville
Saint-Peter's Port
Guernesey
GY1 1DG
Channel Islands
Tel.: + 44 (0) 1481 721 911
Fax: + 44 (0) 1481 715 913
E-mail: hugohouse@cwgsy.net

Opening dates

From April 1st to September 30th, from Monday to Saturday (inclusive French and local holidays).

Hours

April: from 12 a.m. to 4 p.m. (last admission)
From May to September: from 10 a.m. to 4 p.m. (last admission)
Closed on Sundays

Illustrations on the opening pages
The references correspond to the images from left to right and from top to bottom.

Ground floor, p. 24
– Victor Hugo, detail of the drawing of the fireplace in the dinning room, brown ink on paper, 21 x 12.8 cm, glued by Victor Hugo in a notebook named *Dessins ébauchés*, 7.4 x 13 cm, MVHP-D-1393 f° 38
– Julie Duvidal de Montferrier (1797-1869), *Léopoldine au bonnet blanc*, 1825, oil on canvas, 16.5 x 13.5 cm, MHVP-P-330, billiard room (detail)
– Detail of the Dutch stained glass in the studio/smoking room, 17th century
– Detail of the tapestry over the Dutch chest in the studio/smoking room
– Detail of a motif in earthenware stone floor in the Dining room

First floor, p. 44
– Victor Hugo, detail of the drawing of the *porte-torchères* in the red drawing room, brown ink on paper, 10 x 11 cm, glued in a copy of *Chez Victor Hugo par un passant*, Paris, 1864, Cadart and Luquet, MVHP-D-1391-C
– Anonymous, detail of an embroidery representing Açoka, canvas covered with metal, gold and copper, silk and linen, embroidery of glass pearls, 2.25 x 2.42 m, placed by Victor Hugo in the ceiling of the red drawing room
– Detail of a support of the wooden brazier carved and painted by Victor Hugo, 1863
– Detail of a *porte-torchères* in the red drawing room, gilded wood, 18th century, H. 2 m
– Detail of a motif for the wallpaper in the blue drawing room, China, 18th century

Second floor, p. 54
– Victor Hugo, detail of the Oak Gallery, brown ink on paper, 22.1 x 12.4 cm, drawing glued in a copy of *Chez Victor Hugo par un passant*, Paris, 1864, Cadart and Luquet, MVHP-D-1391-J
– Victor Hugo, Hugo de Lorraine family's coat of arms, nails in metal and leather, Garibaldi's room, on a leather bench, D. 72.5 cm, H. 1.31 m, L. 1.45 m
– Victor Hugo, « *Pater* », nails in metal and leather, workroom, back of a leather armchair
– Victor Hugo, Garibaldi's room, the oak gallery
– Initials V.H., engraved and painted wood drawn by Peter Mauger, shutters, Garibaldi's room,

Third floor, p. 64
– Victor Hugo, *Travailleurs de la mer*, manuscript, 1866, MVHP-MS-979 (detail)
– Victor Hugo, detail of the mirror frame placed at the bottom of the staircase leading to the lookout, painting on wood, 1859
– « A.B. », Anne Boleyn's initials on a piece of furniture in the antechamber of the lookout
– *La Princesse*, detail of wood carved and painted by Victor Hugo, a panel in Victor Hugo's room
– Victor Hugo, signature of the pyrographed and painted wooden panels, Victor Hugo's room, 1864

Garden, p. 74
– Victor Hugo, *La Fontaine aux serpents à Hauteville House*, graphite on vellum paper, 45.1 x 28.6 cm, signed with brown ink, pyrographed frame painted with coloured inks, MVHP-D-957
– View of the door of the faience corridor, leading to the garden
– Fu dog, Hauteville House garden
– The « fountain snakes », Hauteville House garden
– Basin of the « fountain snakes »

Written by

Leïla Jarbouai, Curator, Maison de Victor Hugo and Hauteville House
Gérard Pouchain, Professor of History, researcher associated at the University of Rouen, vice-president of the Victor Hugo's friends Society

Acknowledgments

Sheila Gaudon, Honorary Researcher at the CNRS (National Center for Scientific Research), Co-director of the general correspondance of Victor Hugo
Odile Blanchette, Administrator of Hauteville House
Stéphanie Duluc, Guide at Hauteville House
Anne Juin, Curator at the musée Cernuschi
And the teams of Hauteville House and the Maison de Victor Hugo in Paris.

Director of publication
Danielle Molinari

Editorial coordination
at the Maison de Victor Hugo
and Hauteville House
Leïla Jarbouai

Graphic Design
Nicolas Hubert

Editorial coordination
Anne-Julie Esparceil

Translation from French to English
David Wharry

Copyediting
Susan Power

Photographic rights
Laurence Goupille

Production
Saint-Véron Pompée,
Mara Mariano

Colour Separation
Fotimprim, Paris

Printing
Imprimerie Lesaffre

Achevé d'imprimer sur les presses de l'imprimerie Lesaffre, en Belgique, en juin 2010

Diffusion: Actes Sud
Distribution: UD-Union Distribution

ISBN : 978- 27596-0131-8

Dépôt légal : juin 2010

Les musées de la Ville de Paris
28, rue Notre-Dame-des-Victoires
75002 Paris
www.parismusees.com

Photographic credits

© AKG-Images/Olivier Mériel: p. 28, 33 (bottom), 56, 63
© Cédric Bail: p. 24 (middle left)
© Odile Blanchette: cover, 24 (bottom left and right), 44 (middle and bottom left, bottom right), 51, 52, 54 (top right, middle and bottom left), 64 (excepted top left), 74 (excepted top left)
© Direction des Affaires culturelles de la Ville de Paris/Christel Bortoli: p. 71, 77
© Graham Jackson: p. 33 (top), 37, 48 (top), 57
© Gérard Pouchain: p. 21, 50, 60, 68
© Yvette Prigent: p. 4
© André/Maisons de Victor Hugo/Roger-Viollet: p. 11, 59; Edmond Bacot/Maisons de Victor Hugo/Roger-Viollet: p. 41, 76; Françoise Cochennec/Maisons de Victor Hugo/Roger-Viollet: p. 24 (top left), 43; Arsène Garnier/Maisons de Victor Hugo/Roger-Viollet: p. 9, 48 (bottom), 79; Charles Hugo/Maisons de Victor Hugo/Roger-Viollet: p. 12; Philippe Ladet/Maisons de Victor Hugo/Roger-Viollet: p. 42, 44 (top right), 49; Joël Laiter/Maisons de Victor Hugo/Roger-Viollet: p. 35, 46, 58; Maisons de Victor Hugo/Roger-Viollet: p. 6, 10, 17, 22, 24 (top right), 27, 30, 39, 44 (top left), 53, 54 (top left and bottom right), 62, 64 (top left), 66, 69, 72, 73, 74 (top left); Jean-Marc Moser/Maisons de Victor Hugo/Roger-Viollet: p. 26; Stéphane Piera/Maisons de Victor Hugo/Roger-Viollet: p. 36

With the kind collaboration of La Parisienne de Photographie/Roger-Viollet